Ralph Hamor

A True Discourse of the Present Estate of Virginia,

and the successe of the affaires there till the 18 of June 1614.

Ralph Hamor

A True Discourse of the Present Estate of Virginia,
and the successe of the affaires there till the 18 of June 1614.

ISBN/EAN: 9783337222420

Printed in Europe, USA, Canada, Australia, Japan

Cover: Foto ©ninafisch / pixelio.de

More available books at **www.hansebooks.com**

A TRVE DISCOVRSE OF THE PRESENT ESTATE OF VIRGINIA, and the successe of the affaires there till the 18 of *Iune.* 1614.

TOGETHER.

WITH A RELATION OF THE seuerall English Townes and fortes, the assured hopes of that countrie and the peace *concluded with the Indians.*

The Christening of *Powhatans* daughter *and her marriage with an English-man.*

Written by RAPHE HAMOR the yonger, late Secretarie in that Colony.

Alget, qui non ardet.

Printed at London by IOHN BEALE for WILLIAM WELBY dwelling at the signe of the *Swanne in Pauls Church-yard* 1615.

TO THE TRVLY

Honorable and right worthy Knight,

S[r]. *Thomas Smith*, Gouernour of the *East India*, Muscouia, North-west passages, Somer Islands *Companies, and Treasurer for the first Colony in* VIRGINIA.

Honourable Sir :

HAuing in the time of my residence in *Virginia* (as it is true, my imployment then inuited mee thereunto) collected for my owne vse and benefit, some few occurrents and accidents, which are obuious in all new imployments , a thing which perhaps but few regard there to busie themselues with, and fewer heer to peruse : I resolued indeed only to delight my selfe, and some who I am bound to be thankefull vnto in that kinde, with the vnworthy view of them, the rather, because I haue seen many publications & impressions of those affairs, by those, whose books I should be proud to beare after them : but such is the peruersenes of mankinde, such their incredulity of euery thing, saue what their eies tell them to be true : yea, such their backwardnes in the pursuit of honorable enterprises, that though there should be no end of writing, but euery day should drawe foorth his line, and euery line his reall encouragement, as mine may in the state of the Colony, as it now standeth, it were hard to say whether one of so many thousands as abound in *England*, might be thereby moued to ioine with others right worthyly disposed, to become a harty and deuoted furtherer of an action so noble, as is this, which thing if I faile in effecting, I shall not lose much labour, since when I vndertook this taske, I imagined no such thing: but meerly my owne delight and content. It shall be reward enough for me to expresse my indeauours there, though not equall with the best, yet not idly mispent.

I labor not to seduce or betray any into an action or imployment, wherein once personally ingaged, they should haue any cause to blame me, neither would I force the helpe of any mans purse, more then voluntary, if I could beyond my art, vse such effectuall perswasions.

There are enough in my opinion, and those the worthyest of *England* already vnited, as the way is now laid downe, to perfect this businesse, whose indeuours, if they proceed without back slyding, and therein persist some fewe yeers longer, shall be requited and paid with such treble interest, as it shall not repent him that is now most cold in the pursuit, to haue refused more Competitors to be sharers in the returnd profit.

Your noble selfe Sir, euer emulous of vertue, and honourable Enterprises, should shine to the world more noble in the vpholding of this imployment, though it apeared, as in the beginning, full of discouragement, which neuerthelesse

leſſe, I know yourſelfe reſts ſo aſſured is now more neer, than euer to perfection. Your innate and habituall vertue needs no ſpurre, your honourable indeauours well witneſſe the ſame: would God (as is yours) al mens offrings, though not ſo ample, were ſo free, ſo hartily ſacrificed: then could they not thus long haue wanted their rewards, perhaps for no other end detained, but to make others, a thing which God profeſſeth to loue and delight in, more cheerful giuers. Accept (worthy Sir) this vnworthy Treatiſe, the beſt teſtimony of my gratuity, which as yet my diſabilities may render. Trueth ſhall ſhroud and patronize it, from the maleuolent detracting multitude; whoſe blame though it incurre their ſhame and imputation, it ſcorns, and returns vnto them.

My zeale to the Action, though I may ſeeme to haue forſaken it, giues mee the heart to publiſh, what I know, to the world: To your ſelfe particularly your own worth, and deſerts to me, irrequitable, graunt but that fauourable acceptation, which euer accompanies your worth; and I ſhal euer acknowledge my ſelfe wholly yours, in hope wherof I conclude with my ſeruice: & reſt,

At your commaund to be diſpoſed off;

RALPH HAMOR.

To the Reader.

I*Gnorant, or enuious, if you be Readers: it is not to ſatiſfie the beſt of you that I now write, a more ſeaſonable time I muſt take to imbarque my ſelfe in ſo rough a* Sea *and come off ſafe: onely his authoritie (who hath power to compell my ſelfe and duety) hath commaunded me to ſatiſfie his affections (couetous of the dignitie and truth of this pious* Plantation) *with theſe particulars: that they are got abroade, and become publike, was no purpoſe in their firſt conception, though ſome reſpect haue made them ſo now: A naked and vnſtudied* diſcourſe, *I acknowledge, without notes reſerued* (but in Memorie) *to helpe it: yet thus much I doe auow, that it hath duety and truth to make good all other the wants, and imperfections of it, I will labour in no further excuſe.*

Concerning the Virgine *pious worke it ſelfe, how it hath thriued vnder the commaund both of Sir* Thomas Gates *Knight, Gouernour, and Sir* Thomas Dale *Knight, and* Marſhall of the Collonie, *theſe three yeeres and more: let me ſay, if (ſetting aſide thine owne ouerweening and ſingularity) thy vnhooded eye, can now at length looke vpon it (after ſo many yeeres of her patience and paſſions) thou wilt eaſily acknowledge, whoſe finger hath the alone-guidance of it, and then (I doubt nothing) be pleaſed to hea rthy ſelfe intreated (out of thoſe great plenties and hauings which God hath lent thee) to ſpare a little–little portion to the ful ſetling and finiſhing*

vp

vp a Sanctum Sanctorum an holy house, a Sanctuary to him, the God of the Spirits, of all flesh, amongst such poore and innocent seduced Sauages as we treate of, on whom let our hopes be, that it hath vouchsafed him now to be sufficiently reuenged for their forefathers Ingratitude and treasons, and now in his appointed time to descend in mercie, to lighten them that sit in darknes, and in the shadow of death, and to direct their feete in the waies of peace.

Sure, yong though in yeeres and knowledge, I may be said to be, yet let me remember, to thee perhaps much knowing Reader, what the wisest man that euer writ or spake (excepting him that was both God and man) hath said, that such who bring others vnto righteousnesse shal themselues shine as the stars in the firmament. And doubtlesse I doe beleeue, euen amongst the rest of my Articles, when these poore Heathens shall be brought to entertaine the honour of the name, and glory of the Gospell of our blessed Sauiour, when they shall testifie of the true and euerliuing God, and Iesus Christ to be their Saluation, their knowledge so inlarged and sanctified, that without him they confesse their eternal death: I do beleeue I say (and how can it be otherwise?) that they shal breake out and cry with the rapture of so inexplicable mercie: Blessed be the King and Prince of England, and blessed be the English Nation, and blessed foreuer be the most high God, possessor of Heauen and earth, that sent these English as Angels to bring such glad tidings amongst vs. These will be doubtlesse the empaticke effects and exultation of this so Christian worke, and may these nothing moue? Alas let Sanballat and Tobiah, Papists and Plaiers, Ammonites and Horonites, the scumme and dregges of the people, let them mocke at this holy Businesse, they that be filthie, let them be filthie still, and let such swine wallow in the mire, but let not the rod of the wicked fall vpon the lot of the righteous, let not them

shrinke

ſhrinke backe, and call in their helpes from this ſo glorious enterpriſe, which the prophet Iſaiah *cals, the declaring of God to the left hand, but let them that know the worke, reioice and be glad in the happie ſucceſſe of it, proclaiming that it is the euerliuing God that raigneth in* England, *and vnto the ends of the world.*

Excuſe me (curteous reader) if carried beyond my purpoſe, I declaime paſſionately in this paſſiue and innocently deſpiſed worke, which I am ſure is ſo full of goodneſſe, and haue bin almoſt ſix yeers a Sufferer *and eye witnes of his now well nigh atchieued happineſſe, the full and vnſtained reportory of euery accident whereof euen from his beginning, together with the cauſes of the backwardnes, in proſperity thus lōg, touching at the miraculous deliuery of the ſcattered company, caſt vpon the* Bermudas, *when thoſe fortunate Iſlands like ſo many faire Neriades which receiued our wrackt company, with the death of that pure and noble hearted Gentleman Sir* George Sumers *diing there, my purpoſe is ſhortly at large to publiſh, that at length ſome one eſcaped Leaper, amongſt ſo many ſaued, may returne backe and pay his vowes of thanks-giuing vnto that euer to be praiſed mercifull prouidence that brought vs thither, vntil when I wiſh thy zealous and feruent thoughts and indeuours to a buſineſſe ſo full of piety, as is this our* Virginie *Plantation.*

RAPHE HAMOR.

A TRVE DISCOVRSE of the present estate of Virginia, and the successe of the affaires there till the 18 *of Iune.* 1614.

He many publications and impressions of Virginia, an imployment wherein to this day my selfe with many other vnstaid heads & thirstie after new designes, haue bin to vnprofitably ingaged, might iustly excuse my silence, did not the filiall duty whereby in all things to the vtmost of my power I am bound to obey my Father, compell me vnwillingly thereunto: A taske I know by himselfe and others, meerely because I haue bin *Oculatus testis*, thus imposed vpon me, in the vndertaking and performance whereof, I hartily wish that my poore relation, rich onely in truth (as I shall cleerely iustifie my selfe by eie witnesses also) may giue any credit or incouragement to proceede in a businesse so full of honour, and worth, whereunto (if there were no secondary causes) the already publisht ends, I meane the glory of God in the conuerſion of thoſe Infidels. and the honour of our King and country (which by right may claime at the leaſt their ſuperfluities, from thoſe whom God hath in this world made his diſpenſors and purſe-bearers) might be a ſufficient ſpurre to reſolued Chriſtians, eſpecially the ſtate and condition of our collonie. ſo ſtanding when I left it. and I aſſure my ſelfe in this time growne more mature. that an honeſt hart would euen relent, and mourne to thinke how poorely. I dare not ſay vnworthily it is proſecuted. It being true that now after fiue yeeres inteſtine warre with the reuengefull implacable Indians. a firme peace (not againe eaſily to be broken) hath bin lately concluded, not onely with the nighbour. and bordering Indidians, as on *Pataomecke. Topahanah.* and other Riuers, but euen with that ſubtill old reuengefull *Powhatan* and all the people vnder his ſubiection. for all whom *Powhatan* himſelfe ſtands firmely ingaged, by which meanes we ſhall not onely be furniſhed with what commodities their countrie yeeldeth. and haue all the helpes they may afforde vs in our indeuours (as they are eaſily taught. and may by lenitie and faire vſage, as Sir Thomas *Dale* now principall commander there. and moſt worthy the honour he houlds. is well experienced in their diſpoſitions, and accordingly makes vſe of them) be brought . being naturally though ingenious. yet idlely giuē. to be no leſſe induſtrious. nay to exceede our Engliſh, eſpecially thoſe which we hitherto and as yet are furniſhed with. who for the moſt part no more ſenſible then beaſts. would rather ſtarue in idleneſſe (witneſſe their former proceedings) than feaſt in labour, did not the law compell them thereunto, but alſo which will be moſt for our benefit. our owne men may without hazard. I might ſay with ſecurity (by ſelfe-experience) follow their ſeuerall labours, whereby twentie ſhall now

be

bee able to performe more then heretofore hath bin fortie.

Though I coniecture and assure my selfe that yee cannot be ignorant by what meanes this peace hath bin thus happily both for our proceedings and the welfare of the Naturals concluded. yet for the honour of Captain *Argol* whose indeuours in the action intituled him most worthy. I iudge it no whit impertinēt in my discourse to insert them. which w th as much breuity as I may, not omitting the circumstances most pertinent and materiall, I shall indeuour.

The general letters vpon my knowledge. directed and sent to the honourable *Virginia* Councell. being most of them (though my selfe most vnworthy) by me penned, haue intimated, how that the euerworthy gentlemā Capt. *Argall* in the heate of our home furies & disagreements by his best experience of the dispositiō of those people, partly by gentle vsage & partly by the composition & mixture of threats hath euer kept faire & friendly quarter with our neighbours bordering onother riuers of affinity. yea consanguinity. no lesse neere than brothers to *Powhatan*. such is his well knowne temper and discretion. yea to this passe hath he brought them. that they assuredly trust vpon what he promiseth. and are as carefull in performing their mutuall promises, as though they contended to make that *Maxim*. that there is no faith to be held with Infidels. a meere and absurd *Paradox*: Nay as I haue heard himselfe relate. who is *fide dignus*. they haue euen bin pensiue and discontented with themselues. because they knew not how to doe him some acceptable good turne, which might not onely pleasure him, but euen be profitable to our whole Collonie. and *Plantation*, yea euer assuring him that when the times should present occasion, they would take hold of her forelocke, and be the instruments to worke him content, and euen thus they proued themselues as honest performers, as liberall promisers. It chaunced *Powhatans* delight and darling, his daughter *Pocahuntas*, (whose fame hath euen bin spred in England by the title of *Nonparella of Virginia*) in her princely progresse, if I may so terme it, tooke some pleasure (in the absence of Captaine *Argall* (to be among her friends at *Pataomecke*, (as it seemeth by the relation I had) imploied thither, as shopkeepers to a *Fare*, to exchange some of her fathers commodities for theirs, where residing some three months or longer, it fortuned vpon occasion either of promise or profit, Captaine *Argall* to arriue there, whom *Pocahuntas*, desirous to renue hir familiaritie with the English, and delighting to see them, as vnknowne, fearefull perhaps to be surprised, would gladly visit as she did, of whom no sooner had Captaine *Argall* intelligence, but he delt with an old friend, and adopted brother of his *Iapazeus*, how and by what meanes he might procure hir captiue, assuring him, that now or neuer, was the time to pleasure him, if he entended indeede that loue which he had made profession of, that in ransome of hir he might redeeme some of our English men and armes, now in the possession of her Father, promising to vse her withall faire, and gentle entreaty: *Iapazeus* well assured that his brother, as he promised would vse her curteously promised his best indeuours and secresie to accomplish his desire, and thus wrought it, making his wife an instrument (which sex haue euer bin most powerfull in beguiling inticements) to effect his plot which hee had thus laid, he agreed that himselfe, his wife, and *Pocahuntas*, would accompanie his brother to the water side, whether come, his wife should faine a great and longing desire to goe aboorde, and see the shippe, which being there three or foure times, before

fore ſhe had neuer ſeene, and ſhould bee earneſt with her huſband to permit her: he ſeemed angry with her, making as he pretended ſo vnneceſſary a requeſt, eſpecially being without the company of women, which denial ſhe taking vnkindely, muſt faine to weepe (as who knows not that women can command teares) whereupon her huſband ſeeming to pitty thoſe counterfeit teares, gaue her leaue to goe aboord, ſo that it would pleaſe *Pochahuntas* to accompany her: now was the greateſt labour to win her, guilty perhaps of her fathers wrongs, though not knowne as ſhe ſuppoſed to goe with her, yet by her earneſt perſwaſions, ſhe aſſented: ſo forthwith aboord they went, the beſt cheere that could be made was ſeaſonably prouided, to ſupper they went, merry on all hands, eſpecially *Iapazeus* and his wife, who to expres their ioy, would ere be treading vpõ Capt. *Argals* foot, as who ſhould ſay tis don, ſhe is your own. Supper ended, *Pochahuntas* was lodged in the Gunners roome, but *Iapazeus* and his wife deſired to haue ſome conference with their brother, which was onely to acquaint him by what ſtratagem they had betraied his priſoner, as I haue already related: after which diſcourſe to ſleepe they went, *Pocahuntas* nothing miſtruſting this policy. who neuertheles being moſt poſſeſſed with feare, and deſire of returne, was firſt vp, and haſtened *Iapazeus* to be gon. Capt. *Argall* hauing ſecretly well rewarded him, with a ſmall Copper kettle, and ſom other les valuable toies ſo highly by him eſteemed, that doubtleſſe he would haue betraied his owne father for them, permitted both him and his wife to returne, but told him, that for diuers conſiderations, as for that his father had then eigh of our Engliſh men, many ſwords, peeces, and other tooles, which he had at ſeuerall times by trecherons murdering our men, taken from them, though of no vſe to him, he would not redeliuer, he would reſerve *Pocahuntas*, whereat ſhe began to bee exceeding penſiue, and diſcontented, yet ignorant o the dealing of *Iapazeus*, who in outward appearance was no les diſcontented that he ſhould be the meanes of her captiuity, much a doe there was to perſwade her to be patient, which with extraordinary curteous vſage, by little and little was wrought in her, and ſo to *Iames* towne ſhe was brought, a meſſenger to her father forthwith diſpached to aduertiſe him. that his only daughter was in the hands & poſſeſſion of the Engliſh: ther to be kept til ſuch time as he would ranſom her with our men, ſwords, peeces, & other tools treacherouſly taken from vs: the news was vnwelcome, and troubleſom vnto him, partly for the loue he bare to his daughter, and partly for the loue he bare to our men his priſoners, of whom though with vs they were vnapt for any imployment) he made great vſe: and thoſe ſwords, and peeces of ours, (which though of no vſe to him) it delighted him to view, and looke vpon.

He could not without long aduiſe & delibertion with his Councell, reſolue vpon any thing, and it is true, we heard nothing of him till three moneths after. by perſwaſions of others he returned vs ſeauen of our men, with each of them a Musket vnſeruiceable, and by them ſent vs word, that whenſoeuer wee pleaſed to deliuer his daughter, he would giue vs in ſatisfaction of his iniuries done to vs, and for the reſt of our peeces broken and ſtolne from him, 500 Buſhells of Corne, and be for euer friends with vs, the men and Peeces in part of payment we receiued: and returned him anſwere, that his daughter was very well, and kindely intreated, and ſo ſhould be howſoeuer he dealt with vs: but we could not beleeue that the reſt of our Arms were either loſt, or ſtolne from him, and therefore till he returned them all, we would not by any meanes deliuer his daughter,

ter, and then it should be at his choice, whether he would establish peace, or continue enemies with vs. This answere as it seemed, pleased him not very wel, for we heard no more from him till in March last, when with Captaine *Argalls* Shippe. and some other Vessells belonging to the Colony, Sir *Thomas Dale* with an hundred and fifty men well appointed, went vp into his owne Riuer, where his chiefest habitations were, and carried with vs his daughter, either to moue them to fight for her, if such were their courage and boldnesse,, as hath been reported, or to restore the residue of our demands, which were our peeces, swords, tooles. Some of the same men which he returned (as they promised) ran to him again, and because he had put vs to the trouble to fetch them fiue hundred bushels of Corne: A great brauado all the way as we went vp the Riuer they made, demaunding the cause of our comming thither, which wee tould them was to deliuer *Pocahuntas*, whom purposely we had brought with vs, and to receiue our Armes, men, & corn, or else to fight with them, burn their howses. take away their Canoas, breake downe their fishing Weares, and doe them what other damages we could: Some of them to set a good face on the matter, replied, that if wee came to fight with them? we were welcome, for they were prouided for vs, councelling vs rather to retire (if wee loued our safeties) then proceed, bragging, as well they might, that wee had euer had the worst of them in that Riuer, instancing by Capt: *Ratliefe* (not worthy remembring, but to his dishonor) who, with most of his company they betrayed and murthered: we told them since they durst remember vs of that mischief, vnlesse they made the better and more speedy agreement, we would now reuenge that trechery, and with this discourse by the way as we went, we proceeded, and had no sooner entred the narrow of the riuer, the channell there lying within shot of the shoare, but they let their arrowes flie amongst vs in the shippe, themselues vnseene to vs, and in the forehead hurt one of our men, which might haue hazarded his life without the present helpe of a skilfull Chirurgion.

Being thus iustly prouoked, we presently manned our boates, went ashoare, and burned in that verie place some forty houses, and of the things we found therein, made freeboote and pillage, and as themselues afterward confest vnto vs, hurt and killed fiue or sixe of their men, with this reuenge satisfying our selues, for that their presumption in shooting at vs, and so the next day proceeded higher vp the Riuer, the Indians calling vnto vs, and demaunding why we went a shoare, burnt their houses, killed and hurt their men, and tooke away their goods. We replied that though we came to them in peaceable manner, and would haue beene glad to haue receiued our demaunds with loue and peace, yet we had hearts and power to take reuenge, and punish where wrongs shold be offered, which hauing now don, though not so seuerely as we might, we rested content therewith and are ready to imbrace peace with them if they pleased. Many excuses they seemed to pretend, that they shot not at vs, but (if any such abuse were offered) it was some straglcd Indian, ignorant of our pretence in comming to them, affirming that they themselues would be right glad of our loue, and would indeauour to helpe vs to what we came for, which being in the possession of *Powhatan* their King, they would without delay dispatch messengers to him, to know his purpose and pleasure, desiring faire quarter some 24 howers, for so long they pretended it would be before their messengers might returne: this wee graun-

graunted, and what we promised, we euer exactly performed, the time now come, we inquired what *Powhatan* would doe, and had for answere, that our Englishmen lately with him, fearefull to be put to death by vs, were runne away, and some of *Powhatans* men sent abroade in quest of them, but our swords and peeces so many as he had should be brought the next day, which meerely to delay time, they bare vs in hand the next day they came not, higher vp the riuer we went, and ancored neere vnto the chiefest residencie *Powhatan* had, at a towne called *Matchcot* where were assembled (which we saw) about 400 men, well appointed with their bowes and arrowes to welcome vs, here they dared vs to come a shoare, a thing which we purposed before, so a shoare we went, our best landing being vp a high steepe hill which might haue giuen the enemy much aduantage against vs, but it seemed they as we were vnwilling to begin, and yet would gladly haue bin at blowes, being landed as if they had no shew of feare, they stirred not from vs, but walked vp and downe, by and amongst vs, the best of them inquiring for our Weroance or king, with whom they would gladly consult to know the occasion of our comming thither, whereof when they were informed, they made answere that they were there ready to defend themselues, if we pleased to assault them, desiring neuerthelesse some small time to dispatch two or three men once more to their king, to know his resolution, which if not answerable to our requests, in the morning if nothing else but blood would then satisfie vs, they would fight with vs, and thereby determine our quarrell, which was but a further delay to procure time to carrie away their prouisions, neuerthelesse we agreed to this their request, assuring them till the next day by noone we would not molest, hurt, nor detaine any of them, and then before we fought, our Drum and Trumpets should giue them warning: vpon which promise of ours, two of *Powhatans* sonnes being very desirous to see their sister who was there present ashore with vs, came vnto vs, at the sight of whom, and her well fare, whom they suspected to be worse intreated, though they had often heard the contrary, they much reioiced, and promised that they would vndoubtedly perswade their father to redeeme her, and to conclude a firme peace foreuer with vs, and vpon this resolution the two brothers with vs retired aboarde, we hauing first dispatched two English men, Maister Iohn *Rolfe* and maister *Sparkes* to acquaint their father with the businesse in hand, the next day being kindly intreated, they returned, not at all admitted *Powhatans* presence, but spake with his brother *Apachamo*, his successor, one who hath already the commaund of all the people, who likewise promised vs his best indeauors to further our iust requests, and we because the time of the yeere being then Aprill, called vs to our businesse at home to prepare ground, and set corne for our winters prouision, vpon these termes departed, giuing them respite till haruest to resolue what was best for them to doe, with this Prouiso, that if finall agreement were not made betwixt vs before that time, we would thither returne againe and destroy and take away all their corne, burne all the houses vpon that riuer, leaue not afishing *Weere* standing, nor a *Canoa* in any creeke therabout, and destroy and kill as many of them as we could.

Long before this time a gentleman of approued behauiour and honest cariage, maister Iohn *Rolfe* had bin in loue with *Pocahuntas* and she with him, which thing at the instant that we were in parlee with them, my selfe made knowne to Sir Thomas *Dale* by a letter from him, whereby he intreated his aduise and furtherance

therance in his loue, if so it seemed fit to him for the good of the Plantation, and *Pocahuntas* her selfe, acquainted her brethren therewith; which resolution Sir Thomas *Dale* wel approuing, was the onely cause: hee was so milde amongst them, who otherwise would not haue departed their riuer without other conditions.

The bruite of this pretended marriage came soone to *Powhatans* knowledge, a thing acceptable to him, as appeared by his sudden consent thereunto, who some ten daies after sent an olde vncle of hirs, named *Opachisco*, to giue her as his deputy in the Church, and two of his sonnes to see the mariage solemnized, which was accordingly done about the fift of Aprill, and euer since we haue had friendly commerce and trade, not onely with *Powhatan* himselfe, but also with his subiects round about vs; so as now I see no reason why the Collonie should not thriue a pace.

Besides this loue by this meanes with *Powhatan* concluded, it will be worth my paines to run ouer our friendship with our next neighbours, the *Chicohominies* lately confirmed, a lustie and daring people, who haue long time liued free from *Powhatans* subiection, hauing lawes and gouernors within themselues; these people hearing of our concluded peace with *Powhatan*, as the noise thereof was soone bruted abroade, sent two of their men vnto vs, and two fat Bucks for present to our king (for so Sir Thomas *Dale* is generally reputed and termed amongst them) and offered themselues and seruice vnto him, alleadging that albeit in former times they had bin our enemies, and we theirs, yet they would now if we pleased become not onely our trustie friends, but euen King IAMES his subiects and tributaries, and relinquish their old name of *Chicohominies*, and take vpon them, as they call vs the name of *Tossantessas*, and because they haue no principall commander or *Weroance*, they would intreate Sir Thomas *Dale* as King IAMES his deputie to be their supreame head, King and gouernor, and in all iust causes and quarrels to defend them, as they would be ready at all times to aide him, onely their desire was to inioy their owne lawes and liberties, and because himselfe, by reason of his many other imployments, beside the charge he hath of his owne people, may not be alwaies present amongst them, to be gouerned as formerly by eight of the elders and principall men amongst them, as his substitutes and councellers, and euen this was the summe and effect of their embassie. Sir Thomas *Dale* appointed a day to send some men into their riuer, to propose certaine conditions vnto them, whereunto if they assented he would gladly accept of their proffered friendship, and be himself their *Weroance:* and with this answere offering them copper for their venison, which they refused to take, dismissed them.

When the appointed day came, Sir Thomas *Dale* himselfe and Captaine *Argall* with 50 men in a barge and frigot, well appointed, least any trecherie might be intended, set forward to *Chicohominie*, an arme of our riuer some seauen miles from Iames Town, where we found the people according to promise expecting our comming, assembled and met together, who after their best and most friendly manner, bad vs welcome, and because our businesse at home would permit vs but small time of stay with them, they presently sent for their principal men, some of whom were then absent, which hastned vnto vs, & the next morning very early assembled, and sat in counsell about this businesse, Captaine *Argall* (supplying Sir Thomas *Dales* place amongst them, who though there present for some respects, concealed himselfe, and kept aboarde his barge) after long discourse of their former proceedings

ceedings, Captaine *Argall* tould them, that now ſince they had intreated peace and promiſed their loue and friendſhip, hee was ſent vnto them from the great *Weroance* to conclude the ſame, all former iniuries on both ſides, ſet apart and forgotten, which he would doe vpon theſe conditions.

Firſt that they ſhould take vpon them, as they promiſed, the name of *Taſſantaſſes* or Engliſh men, and be King IAMES his ſubiects, and be foreuer honeſt, ſaithfull and truſtie vnto his deputie in their countrie.

Secondly, that they ſhould neuer kill any of our men or cattell, but if either our men or cattle ſhould offend them or runne to them, they ſhould bring them home again, and ſhould receiue ſatisfaction for the treſpaſſe done them.

Thirdly, they ſhould at all times be ready and willing to furniſh vs with three or foure hundred bowmen to aide vs *againſt the Spaniards,* whoſe name is odious amongſt them, for *Powhatans* father was driuen by them from the *weſt-Indies* into thoſe parts, or againſt any other *Indians* which ſhould, contrary to the eſtabliſhed peace offer vs any iniurie.

Fourthly, they ſhall not vpon any occaſion whatſoeuer breake downe any of our pales, or come into any of our Townes or forts by any other waies, iſſues or ports then ordinary, but firſt call, and ſay the *Toſſanteſſas* are there, and ſo comming they ſhall at all times be let in, and kindely entertained.

Fifthly, ſo many fighting men as they haue which may be at the leaſt fiue hundred ſhould yeerely bring into our ſtore houſe, at the beginning of their harueſt two buſhels of corne a man, as tribute of their obedience to his Maieſtie, and to his deputy there, for which they ſhould receiue ſo many Iron *Tomahawkes* or ſmall hatchets.

Lastly, the eight chiefe men which gouerne as fubftitutes and Councellors vnder Sir *Thomas Dale*, fhall at all times fee thefe Articles and conditions duly performed for which they fhall receiue a red coat, or liuery from our King yeerely, and each of them the picture of his Maiefty, ingrauen in Copper, with a chaine of Copper to hang it about his necke, wherby they fhall be knowne to be King IAMES his noble Men: fo as if thefe conditions, or any of them be broken, the offenders themfelues fhall not only be punifhed, but alfo thofe Commaundets, becaufe they ftand ingaged for them.

After thefe Articles were thus propofed, the whole affembly affenting thereunto, anfwered with a great fhout, and noife, that they would readily and willingly performe them all: and immediately began the chiefe of the eight to make an oration to the reft, bending his fpeech firft to the old men, then to the yong men, and in conclufion to the women and children, giuing them thereby to vnderftand the fumme of the propofed conditions: and how ftrictly they were to obferue them: in confideration whereof, he further declared what wee haue promifed to doe for them, not onely ro defend and keepe them from the fury & danger of *Powhatan*, which thing they moft feared, but euen from all other enemies, domefticke, or forraigne, and that we would yeerely by trade furnifh them with *Copper*, *Beades*, *Hatchets*, and many other neceffaries, yea, which liked them beft, that we would permit them to enioy their owne liberties, freedoms, and lawes, and to be gouerned as formerly, by eight of their chiefeft men.

It fhall not be vnneceffarie to infert the occafion (as we imagine) of this their much defired, vnexpected friendfhip, which was queftionleffe fome fodaine feare of *Powhatans* difpleafure, being vnited with vs, now

now able to reuenge their disobedience done vnto him: for you must imagine, these people presuming upon their owne strength and number (in no one place in those parts, which we know, so many togeather) to haue a long time neglected *Powhatan*, and refused, (which the place hath been formerly accutomed, and as his right may challenge the homage and duty of subiects, which they ought to haue performed: to which obedience, fearing our power might compell them, they chose rather to subiect themselues to vs, then being enemies to both, to expose & lay themselues open to *Powhatans* tiranny, & oppression: for this they did chiefely insist vpon, that he was an ill *Weroaules*, full of cruelty, and ininstice, couetous of those things they had, and implacable if they denyed him whatsoeuer he demanded, and for these reasons, desired to be made one people with vs, to curbe the pride and ambition of *Powhatan*, from whom to defend them (they tould vs it would be no breach of peace on our parts, since now they were no longer *Chicohomimes*, or *Naturalls*, of that place, but *Tossantessars*, and King IAMES his subiects, whom we are bound to defend.

So soone as there was an end of speaking, and the peace firmely concluded, and assented vnto, Captaine *Argall* by the guift of eight great peeces of *Copper*, and eight great *Tomahawkes*, bound the eight great men, or Councellors to the exact performance, and keeping of the same, according to the conditions proclaimed, which they very gladly and thankefully accepted, and returned him, as testimonies of their loues, *Venison*, *Turkies*, *Freshfish*, *baskets*, *Mats*, and such like things as they were then furnished with, and so the Councell brooke vp, and then euery man brought to sell to our men *Skinnes*, *boules*, *mats*, *baskets*, *tobacco*, *&c.* and became as familiar amongst

vs,

vs, as if they had been English men indeede.

Thus haue I briefely as the matter would permit, discoursed our established friendship with the *Naturalls*, and the occasions thereof, which I hope will continue so long betweene vs, till they shall haue the vnderstanding to acknowledge how much they are bound to God for sending vs amongst them (then which) what worke would be more acceptable to God, more honourable to our King and counrry?

The greatest, and many enemies and disturbers of our proceedings, and that which hath hitherto deterd our people to addresse themselues into those parts haue been onely two; enmity with the *Naturalls*, and the bruit of famine: one of these two (and that indeede, which was some cause of the other) I haue already remoued, and shall as easily take away the other: howbeit it were too great folly (I might say impudency in me) to auer that there hath raigned no such infection in the Colony, occasioned, meerly by misgouernment, idlenesse, and faction, and chiefely by the absence of the euer worthy Commaunders, Sir *Thomas Gates*, and Sir *George Summers* by the prouidence of God, miraculously wract and saued vpon the hopefull *Sumer* Islands, since my selfe cannot but witnesse) of which I had some tast) in what a miserable condition, we found the Colony at our ariuall there, from the *Bermudas*, not liuing aboue threescore persons therein, and those scarce able to goe alone, of welnigh six hundred. not full ten moneths before: yet now I dare and will boldly affirme to the greatest aduersary of the Plantation, that shall auer the contrary, that there is that plenty of foode, which euery man by his owne industry may easily, & doth procure that the poorest there, & most in want, hath not bin so much pinched with hunger this 4 yeers that if he would take any pains, he knew not

not wher to fetch a good meales meate: and true it is, that euery day by the prouidence, and blessing of God, and their owne industry, they haue more plenty then other, the reason hereof is at hand, for formerly, when our people were fedde out of the common store and laboured iointly in the manuring of the ground, and planting corne, glad was that man that could slippe from his labour, nay the most honest of them in a generall businesse, would not take so much faithfull and true paines in a weeke, as now he will doe in a day, neither cared they for the increase, presuming that howsoeuer their haruest prospered, the generall store must maintain them, by which meanes we reaped not so much corne from the labours of 30 men, as three men haue done for themselues: to preuent which mischiefe heerafter Sir *Thomas Dale* hath taken a new course, throughout the whole Colony, by which meanes, the generall store (apparrell onely excepted) shall not be charged with any thing: and this it is, he hath allotted to euery man in the Colony, three English Acres of cleere Corne ground, which euery man is to mature and tend, being in the nature of Farmers, (the *Bermuda* vndertakers onely excepted) and they are not called vnto any seruice or labor belonging to the Colony, more then one moneth in the yeere, which shall neither be in seede time, or in Haruest, for which, doeing no other duty to the Colony, they are yeerly to pay into the store two barrells and a halfe of Corne: there to be reserued to keep new men, which shall be sent ouer, the first yeere after their arriuall: and euen by this meanes I dare say, our store will be bountifully furnished, to maintain three or foure hundred men, whensoeuer they shall be sent thither to vs, that mony which hitherto hath bin disbursed, to prouide a tweluemoneths victualls, if there were but now

D halfe

halfe so much bestowed in clothes, and bedding, will be such comfort to the men, as euen thereby the liues of many shall not onely be preserued, but also themselues kept in strength and heart, able to performe such businesses, as shall be imposed vpon them: and thus shall also the former charge be well saued, and yet more businesse effected, the action renowned, and more commodity returned to the Merchant, and yet faint for want of encouragement.

Concerning the vndertaking of the *Bermuda* City, a businesse of greatest hope, euer begunne in our Territories there, their Pattent, which I purpose in this Treatise to insert, doth apparantly demonstrate, vpon what termes and conditions they voluntarily haue vndertaken that imployment, how forward that businesse is, in his due place shall bee expressed, onely giue me leaue with as much breuity as I may, least any man should diuert his minde, and be fearefull to aduenture his person thither, for feare of famine and penury, to amplifie a little the plenty there, for if it be true, as most certaine it is, that those whom I haue described vnder the title of Farmers, can pay into our Store, two barrels and a halfe of Corne yeerely. and others who labour eleauen moneths in the generall businesse of the Colony, and but one to prouide themselues victualls, why should any man (if he be industrious) mistrust staruing? if otherwise, for my part, and I thinke all that are ingaged in the Action, and vnderstand the businesse, accord with me heerein, and would not wish his company there. nay they shall much wrong themselues, and the Action. if they doe not withstand such, and deny them passage: for euen they and none else haue been the occasions of the manifould imputations, & disgraces, which *Virginia* hath innocently vndergon, through their defaults: I would therefore by these relations not onely encourage honest and industrious: but also deterre all lasie. impotent, and ill liuers from addressing themseues thither, as being a Country too worthy for them, and altogeather disconsonant to their natures, which must either brooke labour or hazard, and vndergoe much displeasure, punishment, and penury, if they escape a thing which few idlers haue don, the scuruy disease, with which few, or none once infected, haue recouered.

To proceed therefore in my incouragement to painefull people, such as either through crosses in this world, or ract rents, or else great charge of children and family liue heer, and that not without much care and sweat, into extreame pouerty: for those this Countrey hath present remedy: Euerie such person, so well disposed to aduentnre thither, shal soon find the difference between their own, and that Country. The affaires in the Colony, being so well ordered, and the hardest taskes already ouerpast, that whosoeuer (now, or heerafter) shall happily arriue there, shall finde a hansome howse of some foure roomes or more, if he haue a family, to repose himselfe in rent freee, and twelue English Acres of ground, adioyning thereunto, very strongly impailed, which ground is onely allotted vnto him for *Roots*, *Gardaine hearbs*, and *Corne:* neither shall hee need to prouide himselfe, as were wont the first planters, of a yeers prouision of victualls, for that the store there will bee able to affoord him, & vpon these conditions he shall be entertained; He shall haue for himselfe & family, a competent 12 months prouision deliuered vnto him, in which time it must bee his care to prouide for himselfe and family euer after, as those already there, to this end he shall be furnished with necessary tooles of all sorts, and for his better subsistance he shall haue Poultry, and swine, and if he deferue it, a Goate or two, perhaps a Cow giuen him, which once compaft. how happily he may liue, as doe many there. who I am fure will neuer returne, I fubmit to their own future well experienced iudgements.

Now, leaft any man fhould yet reft difcouraged becaufe as yet no mention is made of any other prouifion of victualls. faue onely of bread-corne, whih graunt. it may with labour be competently procured, will affoord but a bare. and miferable liuing, I thinke there is no man fo ignorant to conceiue. that fuch a main continent as is *Virginia*, boundleffe, for ought we haue difcouered. and fo goodly Riuers, no where elfe to be parralled, fhould be more barraine of Cattell. Fifh.and Foule. then other Lands, affuredly they are not: for true it is, that the Land is ftored with plenty and variety of wild beaftes. Lions. Bears. Deere of all forts. (onely differing from ours in their increafe, hauing vfuall, three or foure Fawnes at a time, none that I haue feen or heard off vnder two: the reafon whereof fom of our people afcribe to the vertue of fome graffe or hearb which they eate, becaufe our Goats often times bring foorth three. and moft of them two: for my part I rather impute their fecundiry to the prouidence of God. who for euery mouth prouideh meate, and if this increafe were not, the Naturalls would affuredly ftarue: for of the Deere (they kill as doe wee Beefes in *England*) all the yeer long. neither fparing yong nor olde, no not the Does readie to fawne, nor the yong fawnes, if but two daies ould) *Beauers. Otters, Foxes, Racounes.* almoft as big as a *Fox*. as good meat as a lamb. *hares. wild Cats, muske rats, Squirills* flying, and other of three or foure forts. *Apoffumes*, of the bigneffe and likeneffe of a Pigge. of a moneth ould, a beaft of as ftrange as incredible nature, fhe hath commonly feauen

uen yong ones, ſometimes more and ſometimes leſſe which at her pleaſure till they be a moneth olde or more ſhe taketh vp into her belly, and putteth forth againe without hurt to her ſelfe or them.

Of each of theſe beaſts. the Lion excepted, my ſelfe haue many times eaten. and can teſtifie that they are not onely taſtefull, but alſo wholeſome and nouriſhing foode.

There are foule of diuers ſorts. *Eagles, wilde Turkeis* much bigger then our Engliſh. *Cranes, Herons* white and ruſſet, *Hawkes, wilde Pigeons* (in winter beyond number or imagination, my ſelfe haue ſeene three or foure houres together flockes in the aire. so thicke that euen they haue ſhaddowed the skie from vs) *Turckie Buſſards, Partridge. Snipes. Owles, Swans, Geeſe, Brants, Ducke* and *Mallard, Droeis, Shel Drakes Cormorants, Teale, Widgeon, Curlewes, Puits*, beſides other ſmall birds, as Blacke-birde, hedge ſparrowes, Oxeies. wood peckers, and in winter about Chriſtmas many flockes of *Parakertoths*.

For fiſh the Riuers are plentifiully ſtored, with *Sturgion, Porpaſſe, Baſe, Rockfiſh, Carpe, Shad, Herring, Ele, Catfiſh, Perch, Flat-fiſh, Troute, Sheepes-head, Drummers, Iarfiſh. Creuiſes, Crabbes, Oiſters* and diuerſe other kindes, of all which my ſelfe haue ſeene great quantity taken, eſpecially the laſt summer at *Smiths Iſland*, at one hale, a frigots lading of Sturgion, Baſe and other great fiſh in Captaine *Argals* Sauie: and euen at that very place which is not aboue fifteene miles from *Pointcomfort*, if we had beene furniſhed with ſalt, to haue ſaued it, wee might haue taken as much fiſh as would haue ſerued vs that whole yeere.

Nor are theſe prouicion of bread. fleſh and fiſh, al we haue for ſuſtentation of mans life. behold more change and variety of foode, which our ſoile and climate affordeth, *Carrats, Parsneps, Turneps, Raddish*,

Pumpions (of the west Indie kinde in great abundance, of one feede I haue seen an hundreth, much better then ours and lasting all the yeere) *Cabbadge*, *Parsley*, all manner of pothearbs and other hearbes, *Margerum*, *Time*, *winter-Sauory*, *Lettice Purslaine*, &c, and besides the naturall graine of that Country, as wheate pease and beanes, it did me much good to view our English wheate how forward it was, full eard, of one graine fortie eares or more. a span long, and onely wanting ripening in *mid Iune*, our English pease then ripe, and beanes very forward, and English barly very hopefull, such as mine eies neuer beheld better in England: And if that soile bring forth these things (as can those which haue bin there with me affirme and witnesse) as plentifull and vnchangeable for taste and quantity as England or any other country, why shold any man that hath his limbes, in a peaceable state as is that, so much as dreame of staruing?

To goe yet a little further, I know no one Country yeelding without art or industry so maniefruites sure I am England doth not: wilde grapes in abundance al the woods ouer, their iuice sweete and pleasant in taste, some of them wee haue replanted in a vineyard adioyning to *Henrico*, the quantity of three or foure Akers which were this yeere very plentifully laden, to what perfection they will come, the next returne will aduertise: *Cherries* little inferior to ours, which if replanted may prooue as much better as now they are worse *Pissmien plums* in bygnes and fashion like a *Medlar* of a sliptické quality, other sorts of plummes like to our wheat plums, and in goodnes answerable: great fields and woods abounding with *Strawberies* much fairer and more sweete then ours, *Mulberries* of great bignesse, and about the *Bermuda* Cittie and *Hundirds* thereunto belonging great store thereof, *Maricocks* of the fashion of a Lemmon whose

blossome

blossome may admit comparison with our most delightsome and bewtifull flowers, and the fruite exceeding pleasant and tastfull: *Chesnut-trees* towards the fals as many as oakes, and as fertile, many goodly groues of *Chincomen trees* with a huske like vnto a Chesnut, rawe or boyled, luscious and harty meate: Walnuts of three or foure sorts, whereof there might be yeerely made great quantity of oyles, as vsefull and good as that of Oliues: some filberds I haue seene, Crabbes great store. lesse, but not so sower as ours, which grafted with the *Siens* of English aple trees, without question would beare very good fruite, and we doubt not but to haue the *Siens* enough the next yeere, there being in Sir Thomas *Gates* his garden at Iames town, many forward apple & peare trees come vp, of the kernels set the yeere before.

If all this be not sufficient, loe further incouragement, the collony is already furnished with two hundred neate cattell, as many goates, infinite hogges in heards all ouer the woods, besides those to eurie towne belonging in generall, and euery priuate man, some Mares, Horses & Colts. Poultry great store, besides tame Turkeis, Peacockes and Pigeons plentifully increasing and thriuing there, in no Countrie better.

Of our yong Steeres the next winter we doubt not to haue three or foure Ploughes going, which once compast, we shall in short time be able to repay England the corne they haue lent vs.

If I knew yet any further impediments which might seeme to giue discouragement to aduenture thither, I should as easily remoue them.

Obiect that pleaseth the want of cloathes, so long as there are wilde beasts there, and the beasts haue skinnes on their backes (if the necessity were such) why should not we as doe the naturals, cloath our

selues

selues therewith, it is no worse then our fore-fathers haue worne before vs, and such as will saue vs from the colde in winter, and heate in summer: but admit there were no skinnes or being there, our people disdaine to weare them. If there be any man that hath beene so ill an husband here that he cannot furnish himselfe with a yeeres prouision of apparrell; if I might counsell he should not be suffered to goe thither, for that country is not for him, as for others who can prouide apparrell for the first yeere, I hold him a worse husband then the former, that shall at any time after be worse cloathed then he went ouer: the valuable commoditie of Tobacco of such esteeme in England (if there were nothing else) which euery man may plant, and with the least part of his labour, tend and care will returne him both cloathes and other necessaries. For the goodnesse whereof, answerable to *west-Indie Trinidado* or *Cracus* (admit there hath no such bin returned) let no man doubt. Into the discourse wherof, since I am obuiously entred, I may not forget the gentleman, worthie of much commendations, which first tooke the pains to to make triall thereof, his name M[r] Iohn *Rolfe*, *Anno Domini* 1612, partly for the loue he hath a long time borne vnto it, and partly to raise commodity to the aduenturers, in whose behalfe I witnesse and vouchsafe to holde my testimony in beleefe, that during the time of his aboade there, which draweth neere vpon sixe yeeres, no man hath laboured to his power, by good example there and worthy incouragement into England by his letters, then he hath done, witnes his mariage with *Powhatans* daughter, one of rude education,, manners barbarous and cursed generation, meerely for the good and honour of the Plantation: And least any man should conceiue that some sinister respects allured him hereunto, I haue made bold contrary

trary to his knowledge in the end of my treatise to insert the true coppie of his letter, written to Sir Thomas *Dale* to acquaint him with his proceedings, and purpose therein, the rather to giue testimony to the misconstruing and ill censuring multitude of his integritie, in the vndertaking a matter of so great a consequent, who in my hearing haue not spared to speak their pleasures; his owne letter hits them home, and the better sort, who know to censure iudiciously cannot but highly commend and approue so worthy an vndertaking.

Thus farre I haue applied my selfe to incourage personall Aduenturers: I would gladly now by worthy motiues, allure the heauie vndertakers to persist with alacritie and cheerefulnesse, both for their owne reputations, the honour of God, and their King and Country. The worthier sort, J meane those Nobles and others of that honourable counsell interessed therein, neede no spurre, their owne innate vertues driues them a pace. The Merchant onely wants some feeling and present returne of those commodities which he is perswaded the country affordeth: to them therefore I will addresse my speech, and if I may perswade them to be constant in their proceedings, some small time longer, the benefit will be the greater and the more welcome when it commeth.

It is not for nothing Sir Thomas *Dale*, so noblie without respect to his liuing, to his Lady here in England, past the prefixed time of his resolued returne, yet remaineth there; I am sure if he pleased he might returne with as much honour as any man from thence, I say not more.

I shall little neede, and indeede it were but wast and Idle for me to repeate and mention the commodities, which with onely labour may bee there procured: many Treatises hath them at full. Samples haue beene sent home, and no man disputeth the goodnes,or the quantitie there to be had: take therefore double courage to your selues,and let these two yeeres neglect be restored by a cheerefull and new onset,and for your incouragement reade yet a little further,and view the face of the Colony, euen superficially portraide: see what effects these three yeeres haue wrought.

In *May* 1611 Sir Thomas *Dale*, with a prosperous passage, not full eight weekes arriued there, with him about three hundred people, such as for the present speede,and dispatch could then be prouided, of worse condition then those formerly there, who I sorrow to speake it, were not so prouident, though once before bitten with hunger and pennury, as to put corne into the ground for their winters bread,but trusted to the store, then furnished but with eight months prouisiō. His first care therefore was to imploy al hands about setting of Corne at the two Forts,seated vpon *Kecoughtan*, *Henry* and *Charles*, whereby the season then not fully past,thogh about the end of May,we had there an indifferent Crop of good corn.

This businesse taken order for, and the care and trust of it committed to his vnder officers, to *Iames Towne* he hastened, where the most company were, and their daily and vsuall workes, bowling in the streetes.these he imployed about necessary workes,as felling of Timber,repairing their houses ready to fall vpon their heads,and prouiding pales,posts and railes to impaile his purposed new Towne,which by reason of his ignorance in those parts, but newly arriued there, he had not resolued where to seate. For his better knowledge therefore of those parts, himselfe with an hundreth men, spent some time in discouery, first *Nansamund Riuer*, which in dispight of the Indians,then our enemies,he discouered to the head

head, after that, our owne Riuer, to the fals, where-vpon a high land inuironed with the mayn Riuer, som sixteene or twentie miles, from the head of the Fals, neere to an Indian Towne called *Arsahattocke*, he resolued to plant his new Towne, and so did, whereof in his due place I shall make a briefe relation.

It was no meane trouble to him, to reduce his people, so timely to good order, being of so il a condition as may well witnesse his seuere and strict imprinted booke of Articles, then needefull with all seuerity and extremity to be executed, now much mitigated, for more deserued death in those daies, then do now the least punishment, so as if the law should not haue restrained by execution, I see not how the vtter subuersion and ruine of the Colony should haue bin preuented, witnesse Webbes and Prises designe the first yeere, since that Abbots and others more daungerous then the former, and euen this summer, Coles and Kitchins Plot, with three more, bending their course towards the Southward, to a *Spanish Plantation*, reported to be there, who had trauelled (it being now a time of peace) some fiue daies iourney to *Ocanaboen*, there cut off by certaine Indians, hired by vs to hunt them home to receiue their deserts. So as Sir Thomas *Dale* hath not bin tyranous, nor seuere at all; Indeede the offences haue bin capitall, and the offenders dangerous, incurable members, for no vse so fit as to make examples to others, but the manner of their death may some obiect, hath bin cruell, vnusuall and barbarous, which in deede they haue not bin, witnesse France, and other Countries for lesse offences: what if they haue bin more seuere then vsuall in England, there was iust cause for it, we were rather to haue regard to those whom we would haue terrified, and made fearefull to commit the like offences, then to the offenders iustly condemned, It being true that amongst those people (who for the most part are sencible onely of the bodies torment) the feare of a cruell, painefull and vnusuall death, more restrains them then death it selfe.

Thus much obuiously, I proceede in his indeuours vntill Sir Thomas *Gates* his happie arriuall, which was onely in preparing timber, pales, posts and railes for the present impaling this new Towne to secure himselfe and men from the mallice and trechery of the Indians, in the midst and hart of whom, he was resolued to set downe, but before he could make himselfe ready for that businesse, Sir Thomas *Gates* though his passage more long than vsuall, to second him herein, happily arriued about the second of August, with sixe good Shippes, men, prouisions and cattle, whom as yet not fully discouered, we supposed to be a Spanish fleete, thus induced the rather to beleeue, because in company with him were three *Caruals*, vessels which neuer before had bin sent thither, and now onely for the transportation of the Cattle. It did mee much good, and gaue great courage to the whole company to see the resolution of Sir Thomas *Dale*, now wholy busied (our land fortifications to weake to withstand a forraigne Enemy) in lading our prouisions aboard the two good Shippes, the *Starre* and *Prosperous*, and our own *Deliuerance*, then riding before *Iames* town, aboarde which Shippes, he had resolued to encounter the supposed Enemy, animating his people, not onely with the hope of victory if they readily obeied his direction, but also assuring them that if by these meanes God had ordained to set a period to their liues, they could neuer be sacrificed in a more acceptable seruice, himselfe promising, rather to fire the *Spanish* Shippes with his owne, then either basely to yeelde, or to be taken: and in nothing he seemed so much discontent as that we could not possibly lade aboarde

boarde all our prouisions before (the winde being then very faire) they might haue bin with vs, whilest therefore the rest were labouring their vtmost to lade aboarde our prouisions, hee caused a small shallop to be manned with thirty readie and good shot to discouer directly what Shippes they might be, and withall speede to returne him certaine word, which within three houres they did, assuring him that is was an English fleete, Sir Thomas *Gates* Generall thereof: which newes how welcome it was vnto him, principally because now he doubted not the happie progression of the affaires in hand, let any man (equally with him affected to the good and welfare of the action) iudge and determine.

The worthies being met, after salutation and welcome giuen, and receiued, Sir Thomas *Dale* acquainted Sir Thomas *Gates* both with such businesses as he had affected since his arriuall, and also of his resolution to builde a new Towne, at the *Fales*, which designe and purpose of his, Sir Thomas *Gates* then principall Gouernour in *Virginia*, well approuing, furnished him with three hundred and fiftie men, such as himselfe made choise of, and the beginning of *September* 1611 he set from *Iames* town, and in a day & a halfe, landed at a place where he purposed to seate & builde, where he had not bin ten daies before he had very strongly impaled seuen English Acres of ground for a towne, which in honour of the noble Prince *Henrie* (of euer happie and blessed memory, whose royall heart was euer strongly affected to that action) he called by the name of *Henrico*. No sooner was he thus fenced, and in a manner secured from the Indians, but his next worke (without respect to his owne health or particular welfare) was building at each corner of the towne, very strong and high commanders or watchtowers, a faire and handsome Church, and storehou-

 ses

ſes, which finiſhed he began to thinke vpon conuenient houſes, and lodgings for himſelfe and men, which with as much ſpeede as was poſſible, were more ſtrongly and more handſome then any formerly in *Virginia*, contriued and finiſhed, and euen in foure moneths ſpace, he had made *Henrico* much better and of more worth then all the worke euer ſince the Colonie began, therein done.

I ſhould be to tedious if I ſhould giue vp the accompt of euery daies labour, which therefore I purpoſly omit, and will onely deſcribe the towne, in the very ſtate and perfection wich I left it, and firſt for the ſituation, it ſtandes vpon a neck of very high land, 3 parts thereof inuironed with the main Riuer, and cut ouer betweene the two Riuers. with a ſtrong pale, which maketh the neck of land an iſland. There is in this town 3 ſtreets of well framed howſes, a hanſom Church, and the foundation of a more ſtately one laid, of Brick, in length, an hundred foote, and fifty foot wide, beſide Store houſes, watch houſes, and ſuch like: there are alſo, as ornaments belonging to this Town, vpon the verge of this Riuer, fiue faire Block houſes, or commaunders, wherein liue the honeſter ſort of people, as in Farmes in *England*, and there keepe continuall centinell for the townes ſecurity, and about two miles from the towne into the Main, a Pale of two miles in length, cut ouer from riuer to riuer, garded likewiſe with ſeuerall Commanders, with a great quantity of corne ground impaled, ſufficient if there were no more in the Colony ſecured, to maintain with but eaſiy manuring, and huſbandry, more men, then I ſuppoſe, will be addreſſed thither, (the more is the pitty) theſe 3 yeeres.

For the further enlargement yet of this Town, on the other ſide of the Riuer, by impaling likewiſe: for we make no other fence, is ſecured to our vſe, eſpecially

ally for our hogges to feede in, about twelue English miles of ground, by name, *Hope in faith*, *Coxen-Dale*, secured by fiue Forts, called, *Charity Fort*, *Mount malado*, a *retreat*, or *guest house* for sick people, a high seat, and wholsome aire, *Elzabeth Fort*, and *Fort patience*: and heere hath Mr. *Whitacres* chosen his Parsonage, or Church land, som hundred Acres impaled, and a faire framed parsonage house built thereupon, called *Rocke Hall* of this Towne, and all the Forts thereunto belonging, hath Captaine *James Dauis*, the principall Commaunde, and Gouernment.

I proceed to our next and most hopefull habitation, whether we respect commodity, or security, (which we principally aime at) against forraigne designes, and inuasions, I meane the *Bermuda* Citty. begun about Christmas last, which because it is the neerest adioyning to *Henrico*, though the last vndertaken, I hould it pertinent to handle inthe next place. This Towne, or plantation is seated byland, some 5 miles from *Henrico*, by water fourteene, being the yeer before the habitation of the *Appamatucks*, to reuenge the trecherous iniurie of those people. done vnto vs, taken from them besides all their Corne, the former before without the losse of any, saue onely some few of those Indians, pretending our hurt) at what time Sir *Thomas Dale*, being himselfe vpon that seruice, and duly considering how commodious a habitation and seat it might be for vs, tooke resolution to possesse and plant it, and at that very instant, gaue it the name of the new *Bermudas*, whereunto he hath laid out, and annexed to be belonging to the freedome, and corporation for euer, many miles of Champion, and woodland, in seuerall Hundreds, as the vpper and nether Hundreds, *Rochdale* hundred, *WestsSherly* hundred, and *Digges* his hundred In the nether

nether hundred he first began to plant, and inhabite for that there lyeth the most conuenient quantity of Corne ground, and with a Pale cut ouer from Riuer to Riuer, about two miles long, wee haue securd some eight miles circuit of ground, the most part champion, and exceeding good Corne ground, vppon which pale, and round about, vpon the verge of the Riuer in this Hundred, halfe a mile distant from each other, are very faire houses, already builded, besides diuers other particular mens houses, not so few as fifty, according to the conditions of the pattent graunted them, which who so pleaseth to peruse, shall in the end of my discourse finde it inserted. In this Plantation next to Sir *Thomas Dale* is principal, in the Commaund, Captaine *Georg Yardley*, Sir *Thomas Gates* his lieftenaunt, who se endeauours haue euer deserued worthy commendations in that imployment. *Rochdale* Hundred by a crosse pale, well nigh foure miles long, is also already impaled, with bordering houses all along the pale, in which Hundred our hogges, and other cattell haue twenty miles circuit to graze in securely. The vndertaking of the chiefe Citty deferred till their Haruest be in, which once reaped, all hands shall be imployed theron. which Sir *Thomas Dale* purposeth, and he may with some labour effect his designes, to make an impregnable retreat, against any forraign inuasion, how powrefull so euer.

About fifty miles from this seat, on the other side of the Riuers, is *Iames* towne situate, vpon a goodly and fertile Island: which although formerly scandoled with vnhealthfull aire, we haue since approued as healthfull as any other place in the country: and this I can say by mine own experience, that that corn and gardaine ground (which with much labour beeing when we first seated vpon it, a thick wood) wee haue

haue cleered, and impaled, is as fertile as any other we haue had experience and triall off. The Towne it selfe by the care and prouidence of Sir *Thomas Gates*, who for the most part had his chiefest residence there, is reduced into a hansome forme, and hath in it two faire rowes of howses, all of framed Timber, two stories, and an vpper Garret, or Corne loft high, besides three large, and substantiall Storehowses, ioyned togeather in length some hundred and twenty foot, and in breadth forty, and this town hath been lately newly, and strongly impaled, and a faire platforme for Ornance in the west Bulworke raised: there are also without this towne in the Island, some very pleasant, and beutifull howses, two Blockhouses, to obserue and watch least the Indians at any time should swim ouer the back riuer, and come into the Island, and certain other farme howses. The commaund and gouernment of this town, hath master *Iohn Scarpe*, Liftenant to Captain *Francis West*, Brother to the right Honourable, the Lord *Lawarre*.

From *Iames* towne downewards, some forty and odde miles at the mouth of the riuer, neer *Point Comfort*, vpon *Kecoughtan*, are two pleasant and commodious Forts, *Henrie* and *Charles*, goodly seats, and much corne ground about them, abounding with the commodities of *fish*, *fowle*, *Deere*, and fruits, whereby the men liue there, with halfe that maintenaunce out of the Store, which in other places is allowed: certainly this habitation would bee no whit inferiour to the best we haue there, saue, as yet, with the poore meanes we haue; we cannot secure it, if a forraigne enemy, as we haue iust caus to expect daily should attempt it. And of these Forts, Captain *Georg Web* was lately establishd the principall Commander.

F It

It hath been our greateſt care, and labour hitherto, and yet but theſe three yeers. the former foure meerely miſpent, to compaſſe theſe buſineſſes, which being thus ſetled, and brought to ſuch perfection, as I haue deſcribed, now doth the time approch, that commodity may be expected, and if meanes bee ſent ouer, will aſſuredly be returned. What honeſt ſpirit, hauing hitherto laboured herein, would at the vpſhot (as I may ſo term it) be diſcouraged or deſiſt? I hope none, rather more will be animated, (if need require) to put too their helping hands and purſes.

And euen thus I haue ſhaddowed I hope, without the guilt of tedious, or prolix diſcourſes (as I haue been able) the true condition (though many circumſtances omitted) of *Virginia*, what may the ſubſtance be, when the externall ſhew is ſo forward, ſo glorious.

I haue purpoſely omitted the relation of the Contry commodities, which euery former treatiſe hath abundantly. the hope of the better mines, the more baſe, as Iron, Allom, and ſuch like. Perfectly diſcouered, and made triall off, and ſurely of theſe things I cannot make ſo ample relation, as others, who in the diſcouery of thoſe affaires, haue bin. then my ſelfe more often conuerſant, onely of the hopefull, and marchantable commodities of tobacco, ſilke graſſe, and ſilke wormes: I dare thus much affirme, and firſt of Tobacco, whoſe goodneſſe mine own experience and triall induces me to be ſuch, that no country vnder the Sunne, may, or doth affoord more pleaſant, ſweet, and ſtrong Tobacco, then I haue taſted there, euen of mine owne planting, which, howſoeuer being then the firſt yeer of our triall thereof, wee had not the knowledge to cure, and make vp, yet are ther ſome now reſident there, out of the laſt yeers well obſerued experience, which both know, and I doubt not

not, will make, and returne such Tobacco this yeere, that euen England shall acknowledge the goodnesse thereof.

Now I proceed to the silke grasse which groweth like vnto our flax, I meane not, of that kinde formerly sent ouer, I haue seen, euen of the naturall, and wilde plants, which Captaine *Martin*, who much delighteth in those businesses, hath made, exceeding fine, and exceeding strong silke, and himselfe hath replanted many of the wilde plants this yeere, the silke whereof he purposeth to returne for triall.

The silke wormes sent thither from *England*, in seeds the last winter, came foorth many of them the beginning of *March*, others in *Aprill*, *Maye*, and *Iune*, thousands of them grown to great bignesse, and a spinning, and the rest well thriuing of their increase, and commodity well knowne to be reaped by them, we haue all most assurance (since sure I am) no Country affoordeth more store of *Mulbery* trees, or a kind with whose leafe they more delight, or thriue better.

It may be heere happily expected, that I should giue vp the relation of Captaine *Argalls* particular voyages and indeauours, and euen as in a Plat, demonstrate his Norward discoueries, from which businesse I desire to be excused, partly, because himselfe is best able to make his owne relations, and partly, because my home imployments would not permit me leisure to accompany him, though my selfe desirous, in any of his voyages, whose indeauours, if I should indeauour to make knowne, and publish, could receiue no honour at all by my commendations, or descriptions: much might they be impaired, through my ignorance, or vnskillfullnes to set them foorth: yet cannot I omit to publish to the world, what present reliefe he hath don to the Colony, furnishing vs by two trading voyages, with three and twenty hundred bushels of Corne. into our store deliuered : beside, what he reserued for his mens prouision. what he bestowed vpon well deseruers, and what his men appropriated,

I passe by the benefit of peace in those parts, by reason of his Captiue *Pochahuntas*. concluded established, and will onely name the commoditie by his meanes done vnto vs,in repairing of our weatherbeten boats,and furnishing vs with new. both strong, and vsefull, without whose assistance heerin, vnlesse wee should haue omitted other necessary imployments,I see not how we should haue had passage one to another.

His Norward discoueries towards *Sacadehoc*, and beyond to *Port royall*, *Sancta Crux*, and thereabout may not be concealed: In which his aduentures, if he had brought home no commodity to the Colony, (which yet he did very much, both of apparrell, victualls, and many other necessaries) the honour which he hath done vnto our Nation, by displanting the French, there beginning to seate & fortefie within our limits, and taking of their Ship and Pinnas, which he brought to *Iames* Towne, would haue been reward enough for his paines, and will euer speake loud his honour,and approued valour.

I haue heard it credibly reported, euen from the mouth of Captaine *Argall*, that in one small Shippe, and in one voyage, the French haue cleered eight thousand pounds by trade with the Indians, for furs, which benefit wil be as easily by vs procured.

It is true the *Saluadges* there inhabiting (before Captaine *Argalls* arriuall) esteemed the French as Demy-Gods,and had them in great estimation : but seeing them vanquished and ouercom by vs,forsook them, yea, which is no meane point of pollicy, desi-

red

red our friendſhip, telling Captaine *Argall.* that hee had vndone them for euer, for that the French by yeerely trade with them for Furres, furniſhed them with many neceſſaries. whereof they had great want, which trade by this meanes might happily be hindered. But Captaine *Argall* hath agreed with them to reſerue there Furres for him. and promiſed them, once a yeere to come thither, and truck with them: they ſeemed very well content. aſſuring him. that though the French ſhould at any time arriue there, and proffer them trade, they would reſerue all their Furs for him. and what profit by this meanes onely, may be returned to the *Virginia* aduenturers, I ſubmit to Captaine *Argalls* owne oppinion and iudgement.

I purrpoſely omitted one thing in the Trea tiſe of our concluded peace, wherewith I intend to conclud my diſcourſe, which already I haue drawne to a longer period then I purpoſed. whereby wee haue gathered the better aſſurance, of their honeſt inward intentions, and this it is.

It pleaſed Sir *Thomas Dale* (my ſelfe being much deſirous before my returne for *England*, to viſit *Powhatan*, & his Court, becauſe I would be able to ſpeak ſomwhat thereof by mine own knowledge) to imploy my ſelfe. and an engliſh boy for my Interpreter on *Thomas Saluage* (who had liued three yeers with *Powhatan*, and ſpeakes the langauge naturally, one whom *Powhatan* much affecteth) vpon a meſſage vnto him. which was to deale with him, if by any meanes I might procure a daughter of his, who (*Pochahuntas* being already in our poſſeſſion) is generally reported to be his delight, and darling, and ſurely he eſteemeth her as his owne ſoule) for ſurer pledge of peace.

I departed the fifteenth of May early in the mor-

ning

ning, with the English Boy, and two Indian guides, from the Bermudas, and came to his court or residence (as I iudge some three score miles distant from vs, being seated at the head almost of *Pamaunkie* Riuer, at a towne called *MatchCot*) the next night after, about twelue of the clocke, the former night lodging in the open woods, feareles and without daunger: when we were come opposite to his Towne, the maine riuer betweene him and vs, least at any time we should martch by land vnto him vndiscouered: my Indian guides called for a Canoa (a boate made onely of one tree, after the fashion of a hollow trough) to transport vs, giuing them to know that there was two English sent vpon businesse to *Powhatan* from the English *Weroance*, which once knowne, a Canoa was presently sent, and we ferried ouer, *Powhatan* himselfe attending at the landing place to welcome vs. His first salutation was to the Boy, whom he very wel remembred, after this manner: my childe you are welcome, you haue bin a straunger to me these foure yeeres, at what time I gaue you leaue to goe to *Paspahae* (for so was Iames towne called before our seating there) to see your friends, and till now you neuer returned: you (said he) are my child, by the donatiue of Captaine *Newport*, in liew of one of my subjects *Namontacke*, who I purposely sent to King Iames his land, to see him and his country, and to returne me the true report thereof, he as yet is not returned, though many ships haue arriued here from thence, since that time, how ye haue delt with him I know not? hauing thus ended his speech to him, he addressed himself to me, and his first salutation, without any words at all, was about my necke, and with his hand he feeled round about it, so as I might haue imagined he would haue cut my throate, but that I knew he durst not, he asked me where the chaine of

pearle

pearle was, I demaunded what chaine: that, said he, which I sent my Brother Sir *Thomas Dale* for a present. at his first arriuall; which chaine, since the peace concluded, he sent me word, if he sent any Englishman vpon occasion of busines to me, he should weare about his necke, otherwise I had order from him to binde him and send him home againe. It is true Sir *Thomas Dale* had sent him such word (which till then my selfe neuer heard of) and for this purpose had giuen his Page order to deliuer me the said chaine, who forgot it: I was doubtfull at the first how to answere him, yet presently I replied that I was not ignorant of that message from his brother, formerly sent vnto him, whereby he onely entended that if vpon extraordinary and sudden occasion, he should be constrained to send an Englishman vnto him without an Indian guide, then in testimonie that he sent him hee should weare the chaine about his necke: but in case any of his owne people should conduct any English vnto him, as did me, two of his owne men, one of them a Councellor vnto him, who was acquainted with my businesse, their testimony should be sufficient, and the chaine then needelesse to be worne, which answere pleased him well, and fourthwith he brought vs to his house, not full a stones cast from the waterside, whereinto being come, himselfe sat downe on his bedsteade side, bed there was none more then a single mat, on each hand of him was placed a comely and personable young woman, not twenty yeeres old the eldest, which they call his Queenes, the house with in round about bee set with them, the outside guarded with an hundred bowmen, with their quiuers of arrowes at their backes, which at all times, & places attend his person.

The first thing hee offered vs was a pipe of Tobacco, which they call *Pissimore*, whereof himselfe first

first dranke, and then gaue it me, andwhen I had drank what I pleased, I returned his pipe, which with his owne hands he vouchsafed to take from me: then began he to inquire how his Brother Sir *Thomas Dale* fared, after that of his daughters welfare, her mariage, his vnknowne sonne. and how they liked. liued and loued together: I resolued him that his brother was very well.and his daughter so well content that she would not change her life to returne and liue with him, whereat he laughed heartily, and said he was very glad of it. Now proceede (said he) to deliuer the cause of your vnexpected comming; I certified him my message was priuate, to be deliuered to himselfe, without the presence of any.saue one of his Councellers, by name *Pepaschicher*, one of my guides, who was acquainted with my businesse, he instantly commanded all, both men and women out of the house, his two Queenes onely excepted.who vpon no occasion whatsoeuer, may sequester themselues. Now (said he) speake on, and my selfe by my interpreter thus begun. Sir *Thomas Dale* your Brother, the principal commander of the English men, sends you greeting of loue and peace, on his part inuiolable, and hath in testimonie thereof(by me sent you a worthie present, *vid.* two large peeces of copper, fiue strings of white and blew beades, fiue wodden combes, ten fish-hookes and a paire of kniues, all which I deliuered him, one thing after another, that he might haue time to view each particular: He willed me also to certifie you, that when you pleased to send men, he would giue you a great grinding stone: my message and gift hitherto pleased him, I proceeded thus. The bruite of the exquesite perfection of your yongest daughter, being famous through all your territories, hath come to the hearing of your Brother Sir *Thomas Dale*, who for this purpose hath addressed me hither

ther, to intreate you by that brotherly friendſhip you make profeſſion of, to permit her(with me)to returne vnto him,partly for the deſire which himſelfe hath,and partly for the deſire her ſiſter hath to ſee her of whom, if fame hath not bin prodigall, as like enough it hath not, your brother (by your fauour) would gladly make his neereſt companion, wife and bedfellow (many times he would haue interrupted my ſpeech, which I intreated him to heare out, and then if he pleaſed to returne me anſwere)and the reaſon hereof is, becauſe being now friendly and firmely vnited together, and made one people (as he ſuppoſeth and beleeues)in the band of loue,he would make a naturall vnion betweene vs, principally becauſe himſelfe hath taken reſolution to dwel in your country ſo long as he liueth, and would therefore not only haue the firmeſt aſſurance hee may, of perpetuall friendſhip from you, but alſo hereby binde himſelfe thereunto.

When I had thus made an end of ſpeaking; the ſooner by his often interruption, I had no neede to require his anſwere; which readily, and with no leſſe grauity he returned thus.

I gladly accept your Kings ſalute of loue & peace, which while I liue I ſhall exactly, both myſelfe and ſubiects maintaine and conſerue: his pledges thereof I receiue with no leſſe thankes, albeit they are not ſo ample ; howbeit himſelfe a greater *Weroance*, as formerly Captaine *Newport*, whom I very well loue, was accuſtomed to gratefie me with. But to the purpoſe,my daughter whom my brother deſireth, I ſould within theſe few daies to be wife to a great *Weroance* for two buſhels of *Roanoake*(a ſmall kinde of beades) made of oyſterſhels, which they vſe and paſſe one to another, as we doe money (a cubites length valuing ſixe pence)and it is true ſhe is already gone with him, three daies iorney from me. I replied that I knew his greatnesse and power to be such, that if he pleased heerein to gratifie his Brother hee might, restoring the *Roanoake* without the imputation of Iniustice, take home his daughter againe, the rather because she was not full twelue yeeres old, and therefore not marriageable: assuring him beside the band of peace, so much the firmer he should haue treble the prise of his daughter, in beades, Copper, Hatchets and many other things more vsefull for him? his answere hereunto was, that he loued his daughter as deere as his owne life, and though he had many Children, he delighted in none so much as in her, whom if he should not often beholde, he could not possibly liue, which she liuing with vs he knew he could not, hauing with himselfe resolued vpon no termes whatsoeuer to put himselfe into our hands, or come amongst vs, and therefore intreated me to vrge that suite no further, but returne his brother this answer.

I desire no firmer assurance of his friendship, then his promise which he hath already made vnto mee; from me, he hath a pledge, one of my daughters, which so long as she liues shall be sufficient, when she dieth he shall haue another childe of mine, but she yet liueth: I holde it not a brotherly part of your King, to desire to bereaue me of two of my children at once; further giue him to vnderstand, that if he had no pledge at all he should not neede to distrust any iniurie from me, or any vnder my subiection, there haue bin too many of his and my men killed, and by my occasion there shall neuer bee more, I which haue power to performe it, haue said it: no not though I should haue iust occasion offered, for I am now olde, and would gladly end my daies in peace, so as if the English offer me iniury, my country is large enough, I will remoue my selfe farther from you. Thus much

I

I hope will satisfie my brother. Now because your selues are wearie, and I sleepie, we will thus end the discourse of this businesse. Then called he one of his men and willed him to get some bread for vs, himselfe the meane while telling vs that they not expecting our comming, as vsually they doe eate vp all their other victuals, presently the bread was brought in two great wodden bouls, the quantity of a bushel sod breade made vp round, of the bignesse of a tenise ball, whereof we eate some few, and disposed the rest to many of his hungrie guarde which attended about vs: when we had eaten he caused to be fetched a great glasse of sacke, some three quarts or better, which Captain *Newport* had giuen him sixe or seauen yeeres since, carefully preserued by him, not much aboue a pint in all this time spent, and gaue each of vs in a great oister shell some three spoonefuls; and so giuing order to one of his people to appoint vs a house to lodge in, tooke his leaue for that night, and we departed. We had not bin halfe an houre in the house before the fleas began so to torment vs that wee could not rest there, but went forth, and vnder a broade oake, vpon a mat reposed our selues that night no sooner were we awakt and vp in the morning, but *Powhatan* himselfe came to vs, and asked vs how we fared, and immediately led vs to his house, where was prouided for our breakefast a great bole of *Indian* pease and beanes boyled together, and as much bread as might haue sufficed a dosen hungry men, about an houer after boyled fresh fish, and not long after that roasted Oysters, Creuises and Crabbes his men in this time being abroade a hunting some venison, others Turkeis and such like beasts and foule as their woods afforde, who returned before ten of the clocke with three does and a bucke, very good and fat venison, and two great cocke Turkeis, all which were dreſſed that day, and ſupper ended, ſcarce a bone to be ſeene.

Whiles I yet remained there, by a great chaunce came an Engliſhman thither, almoſt three yeeres before that time ſurpriſed, as he was at worke neere *Fort Henrie*, one *William Parker* growen ſo like both in complexion and habite to the *Indians*, that I onely knew him by his tongue to be an Engliſhman, he ſeemed very ioyfull ſo happily to meete me there. Of him when we often inquired, the *Indians* euer tolde vs that he fell ſicke and died, which till now we beleeued: he intreated me to vſe my beſt indeuours to procure his returne, which thing I was purpoſed ſo ſoone as I knew him, and immediately went with him to *Powhatan*, and tolde him that we credibly beleeued that he was dead, but ſince it was otherwiſe I muſt needes haue him home, for my ſelfe of neceſſitie muſt acquaint his brother that I had ſeene him there: who if he returned not, would make another voyage thither purpoſely for him: *Powhatan* ſeemed very much diſcontent, and thus replied. You haue one of my daughters with you, and I am therewith well content, but you can no ſooner ſee or know of any Engliſh mans being with me, but you muſt haue him away, or elſe breake peace and friendſhip: If you muſt needes haue him, he ſhal goe with you, but I will ſend no guides along with you, ſo as if any ill befall you by the way, thanke your ſelues. I anſwered, that rather then I would goe without him, I would goe alone, the way I knew well enough, and other daungers I feared not, ſince if I returned not ſafely, he muſt expect our reuenge vpon him and his people, giuing him further to know, that his brother our king might haue iuſt occaſion to diſtruſt his loue to him, by his ſlight reſpect of me, if he returned mee home without guides. He replied not hereunto, but

in

in passion and discontentment from me, not till suppertime speaking any more vnto me: when sending for me, he gaue me share of such cates as were for himselfe prouided, and as good aspect and countenance as before; but not a word concerning my returne, till himselfe at midnight comming to me, and the boy where we lay awaked vs, and tolde me that *Pepaschechar* and another of his men, in the morning should accompany vs home, earnestly requesting me to remember his brother to send him these particulars. Ten peeces of Copper, a shauing knife, an iron frow to cleaue bordes, a grinding stone, not so bigge but four or fiue men may carry it, which would be bigge enough for his vse, two bone combes, such as Captaine *Newport* had giuen him; the wodden ones his own men can make: an hundred fish-hookes or if he could spare it, rather a fishing saine, and a cat, and a dogge, with which things if his brother would furnish him, he would requite his loue with the returne of skinnes: wherewith he was now altogether vnfurnished (as he tolde me) which yet I knew hee was well stored with, but his disposition mistrustfull and ielous loues, to be on the surer hand.

Whē he had deliuered this his message, he asked me if I will remembred euery paticular, which I must repeat to him for his assurance, & yet still doubtful that I might forget any of them, he bade me write them downe in such a Table book as he shewed me, which was a very fair one, I desired him, it being of no vse to him, to giue it mee: but he tolde me, it did him much good to shew it to strangers which came vnto him: so in mine owne Table booke, I wrot downe each particular, and he departed.

In the morning, himselfe and wee were timely stirring to be gone: to breakefast first we went, with a good boyled Turkie, which ended, he gaue vs a whole Turkie, besides that we left, and three baskets of bread to carry vs home, and when we were ready to depart, hee gaue each of vs an excellent Bucks skin, very well dressed. and white as snow, and sent his sonne and daughter each of them one, demaunding if I well remembred his answer to his brother, which I repeated to him: I hope (said he) this will giue him good satisfaction, if it doe not I will goe three daies iourny farther from him, and neuer see *English* man more: if vpon any other occasion hee send to me again, I wil gladly entertain his messengers and to my powre accomplish his iust requests: and euen thus himselfe conducting vs to the water side, he tooke leaue of vs, and we of him: and about ten of the clock the next night after, we were come to the *Bermudas.* This discourse I haue briefely as I could, and as the matter would permit, the rather related, to make knowne, how charie *Powhatan* is, of the conseruation of peace, a thing much desired, and I doubt not right welcom newes, to the vndertakers heer) as may appeare by his answeres to my requests, and also by my safe passage thither, & homwards, without the lest shew of iniury offred vnto vs, though diuers times by the way, many stragling Indians met vs, which in former times, would gladly haue taken so faire occasion to worke their mischiefe and bloody designes vpon vs. By all which, as likewise by our forward progression in our affaires. I hope such good successe and benefit to bee speedily reaped, that my selfe, though I blesse GOD for it, who hath so prouided for me. that I may liue more happily heere, then many who are fearefull to aduenture thither) could euen willingly make a third voyage thither if by my poore endeauours the businesse might receiue the least furtherance. God, (I hope) will raise vp meanes beyond mans imagina-

tion,

tion, to perfect his owne glory and honour, in the conuersion of those people, of whom vndoubtedly, (as in all other parts in the world,he hath predestinated some to eternall saluation. and blessed shall those be that are the instruments thereof) I hope this poor Narration will moue euery honest heart, to put his helping hand thereunto. For my part,as I haue been fiue yeers a personall workeman in that building,so shall I euer,as my meanes may permit me, be ready to offer my mite towards the furnishing of others, and againe(if need require) personally labor therein.

To the Reader.

THere be two properties eſpecially remarkeable, which ſhould moue all men earneſtly and conſtantly, with all their meanes and endeuour, to deſire the atcheiuing of any thing, and bringing of the ſame vnto perfection: firſt the worth and excellencie: ſecondly the durableneſſe and continuance thereof. For as that thing which is not durable, by reaſon of fragilitie and fugacitie, is not vſually eſteemed of men, though it be excellent: ſo that likewiſe which is not precious, is worthely little regarded, though it be neuer ſo durable. Now the Virginian plantation hath both theſe notable properties, if at the leaſt we will, and impeach them not our ſelues; for what is more excellent, more precious and more glorious, then to conuert a heathen Nation from worſhipping the diuell, to the ſauing knowledge, and true worſhip of God in Chriſt Ieſus? what more praiſeworthy and charitable, then to bring a ſauage people from barbariſme vnto ciuillitie? what more honourable vnto our countrey, then to reduce a farre disioyned forraigne nation, vnder the due obedience of our dread Soueraigne the Kings Maieſtie? what more conuenient then to haue good ſeates abroade for our euer flowing multitudes of people at home? what more profitable then to purchaſe great wealth, which moſt now adaies gape after ouer-greedily? All which benefits are aſſuredly to bee had and obtained by well and plentifully vpholding of the plantation in Virginia. And for the durableneſſe of all

theſe

these great and singular blessings, there can (by Gods assistance) be no doubt at all made, if men's hearts vnto whom God hath lent abilitie) were but inlarged cheerefully to aduenture and send good companies of honest industrious men thither with a mind to inlarge Christs *kingdome: for then will God assuredly maintaine his owne cause. But alas, as there was neuer yet any action so good, so honourable, so glorious, so pious and so profitable, but hath had checkes and discouragements, both by open enemies abroade, and intestine aduersaries at home with in it owne bowels: euen so may I truely say, hath this most glorious, most honourable, most pious and most profitable enterprise had. For as of old, when* Zerubbabell, Ezra *and* Nehemia *returned from* Babell. *by allowance of the king of* Persia *to* Ierusalem, *and began to repaire the walles thereof and to restore Gods seruice, there wanted not a* Sanballat *and others to say:* what doe these weake Iewes? will they fortifie themselues? *will they sacrifice? will they finish it in a day?* Noe, *for* although they builde, yet if a fox goe vp, he shall euen breake downe that stony wall, *Euen so deale many* Sanballates *and* Tobiahes, *forraigne and domesticall enemies of this most religious worke: yea there be many who will not seeme enemies thereunto, but yet will neither further the businesse themselues, no not according to their owne ingagements which in conscience and credite they ought) nor quietly suffer others that otherwise wold, but discourage them therein all they may som saying as* Iudah *once did.* The strength of the bearers is weakned, and there is much earth, so as we are not able to builde the wall. *Som saying with the vnfaithfull* Spies, *sent forth to search the land of* Canaan: The land wee went through to search it out, is a land that eateth vp the inhabitants thereof, for all the people we saw in it are strong, and men of great stature: *yea and some others say, there is much already expended, and yet no*

 profit

profit ariseth, neither is there victuals to be had, for the preseruing of life and soule together. But oh my deere countrie-men, be not so farre bewitched herewith as to be still discouraged thereat for those that bring a vilde slañder vpon this action, may die by a plague before the Lord, as those men did: but rather remembring your auncient worth, renowne, valour and bounty, harken vnto Caleb *and* Iosua. *who stilled the peoples mourning: saying,* Let vs goe vp at once and possesse it, for vndoubtedly we shall ouercome it; *yet not so much now by force of armes as the* Israelites *did then by warrant from God (nor by vtterly destroying of them, as some haue cruelly done since) as by gentlenesse, loue, amity and* Religion. *As for profit it shall come abundantly, if we can with the husband-man, but freely cast our corne into the ground, and with patience waite for a blessing. And of victuals, there is now no complaint at all, and that which was hapned by the meere lasie negligence of our owne people.*

Now to the end that you may the better perceiue these things to be true, & be thereby the more animated cheerefully to goe forward in the vpholding of this holy worke, I will no longer detaine you from the perusall of some Calebs *and* Iosuahs *faithfull reports (writ there in Iune last this present yeere 1614. and sent hither by the last shippe that came thence (for further incouragement to put hereunto speedily & plentifully your helping hands with al alacrity: As for thē that are able, & yet wil not further but indaunger the vtter ruining of this so glorious a cause (by their miserablenesse (being without loue and charitie) to the great dishonour of* God, *and our Countries perpetuall shame should it now sinke, and fall to the ground: I leaue them to him that made them, to dispose of them according to his infinite wisdome. And so come to the letters themselues: the first and chiefest whereof is from Sir* Thomas Dale, Marshall and Gouernour of Virginia, *vnto a* Minister *of London.*

To

To the R. and my moſt eſteemed *friend Mr. D. M. at his houſe at* F. Ch. in London.

R*Ight Reuerend Sr. by Sr.* Thomas Gates *I wrot vnto you, of ſuch occaſions as then preſented themſelues, and now again by this worthy Gentleman Captaine* Argall *I ſalute you: for ſuch is the reuerend regard I haue of you, as I cannot omit any occaſion to expres the ſincere affection I beare you. You haue euer giuen me encouragements to perſeuer in this religious* Warfare,*vntill your laſt Letters; not for that you are now leſſe well affected thereunto: but becauſe you ſee the* Action *to bee in danger by many of their non performances who vnder tooke the buſineſſe. I haue vndertaken,and haue as faithfully,& with all my might indeauored the proſecution with all allacrity, as God that knoweth the heart,can beare me record,what recompence,or what rewards,by whom,or when I know not where to expect; but from him in whoſe* vineyard *I labor, whoſe* Church *with greedy appetite I deſire to erect. My glorious maſter is gone,that would haue ennamelled with his fauours the labours I vndertake, for* Gods cauſe,*and his* immortall *honour. He was the great* Captaine *of our* Iſraell, *the hope to haue builded up this heauenly new* Ieruſalem *he interred(I think) the whole frame of this buſineſſe, fell into his graue: for moſt mens forward (at leaſt ſeeming ſo) deſires are quenched, and* Virginia *ſtands in deſperate hazard.*

You there doe your duties, I will no way omit mine, the time I promiſed to labour, is expired: it is not a yoke of Oxen hath drawn me from this feaſt: it is not the marriage of a wife maks me haſt home, though that ſallat giue an appetite to cauſe me returne. But I haue more care of the Stock, *then to ſet it vpon a die, and rather put my ſelfe to the curteſie of noble & worthy cenſures then ruine this worke; and haue a* iury (*nay a million*) *of foule mouthed detracters, ſcan vpon my endeauours, the ends whereof they cannot diue into. You ſhall briefely vnderſtand, what hath betide ſince my laſt, and how we now ſtand, and are likely to grow to perfection, if we be not altogeather neglected, my ſtay grounded vpon ſuch reaſon, as had I now returned, it would haue hazarded the ruine of all.*

Sir Thomas Gates *hauing imbarqued himſelfe for* England, *I put my ſelfe into Captaine* Argalls *ſhip, with a hundred and fifty men in my frigot, and other boats went into* Pamaunkie *riuer, where* Powhatan *hath his reſidence, and can in two or three daies, draw a thouſand men togeather, with me I carried his daughter, who had been long priſoner with vs, it was a day or two before we heard of them: At length they demaunded why we came; I gaue for anſwere that I came to bring him his daughter, conditionally he would (as had been agreed vpon for her ranſome) render all the armes, tooles, ſwords, and men that had runne away, and giue me a ſhip full of corne, for the wrong he had done vnto vs: if they would doe this, we would be friends, if not burne all. They demaun-*

maunded time to ſend to their King; I aſſented, I taking,they receiuing two pledges, to carrie my meſſage to Powhatan. *All night my two men lay not far from the water ſide,about noon the next day they told them the great* King *was three daies iourney off, that* Opochankano *was hard by, to whom they would haue had them deliuer their meſſage, ſaying, that what he agreed vpon and did, the great King would confirme. This* Opocankano *is brother to* Powhatan, *and is his and their chiefe* Captaine: *and one that can as ſoone(if not ſooner)as* Powhatan *commaund the men. But my men refuſed to doe my meſſage vnto any ſaue* Powhatan, *ſo they were brought back,and I ſent theirs to them,they tould me that they would fetch* Simons *to me, who had thrice plaid the runnagate,whoſe lies and villany much hindred our trade for corne: But they delayed vs,ſo as we went aſhore they ſhot at vs, we were not behinde hand with them,killed ſome,hurt others,marched into the land,burnt their houſes,tooke their corne,and quartered all night aſhore.*

The next day we went further vp the riuer,they dogged vs and called to know whither we went; wee anſwered,to burne all,if they would not doe as we demaunded, and had been agreed vpon. They would they ſaid, bring all the next day,ſo wee forbare all hoſtility, went aſhore, their men in good numbers comming amongſt vs. but we were very cautious, & ſtood to our arms. The Kings daughter went aſhore, but would not talke to any of them ſcarce to them of of the beſt ſort,and to them onely, that if her father

had

had loued her, he would not value her lesse then olde swords,peeces,or axes: wherefore she would stil dwel with the English men, who loued her. At last came one from Powhatan, *who tould vs,that* Simons *was run away,to* Nonsowhaticond,*which was a truth, as afterwards appeared, but that the other English man was dead,that proued a lie: for since,M*[r]. Hamor,*whom I employed to* Powhatan *brought him to mee,our peeces,swords,and tooles within fifteen daies, should be sent to* Iames *towne, with some corne, and that his daughter should be my childe,and euer dwell vvith mee, desiring to be euer friends, and named such of his people, and neighbour Kings,as he desired to be included, and haue the benefit of the peace, promising if any of our men came to him, vvithout leaue from me, he would send them back: and that if any of his men stole from vs, or killed our cattel,he vvould send them to vs to bee punished as vve thought fit. With these conditions we returned, and vvithin the time limited, part of our Arms vvere sent, and* 20. *men vvith corne, and promised more, vvhich he hath also sent.* Opachankano *desired I vvould call him friend,and that he might call me so,saying he vvas a great* Captaine,*and did alwaies fight: that I vvas also a great* Captaine, *and therefore he loued mee; and that my friends should be his friends. So the bargain vvas made, and euery eight or ten daies, I had messages and presents from him, vvith many apparances that he much desireth to continue friendshippe.*

Novv may you iudge Sir, if the God of battailes haue not a helping hand in this, that hauing our swords,

swords drawn, killing their men, burning their houses, and taking their corne: yet they tendred vs peace, and striue with all allacrity to keep vs in good oppinion of them; by which many benefits arise vnto vs. First, part of our Armes, disgracefully lost long agoe, (*kept by the* Sauages *as* Monuments *and* Trophies *of our shames*) *redeliuered, some repaire to our honor. Our catle to increase, without danger of destroying, our men at liberty, to hunt freely for venison, to fish, to doe any thing else, or goe any whither, without danger; to follow the husbanding of their corne securely, whereof we haue aboue fiue hundred Acres set, and God be praised, in more forwardnesse, then any of the Indians, that I haue seene, or heard off this yeere, roots, and hearbs we haue in abundance; all doubt of want is by Gods blessing quite vanished, and much plenty expected. And which is not the least materiall, we may by this peace, come to discouer the countrey better, both by our own trauells, and by the relation of the* Sauages, *as we grow in familiarity with them.*

Powhatans *daughter I caused to be carefully instructed in Christian Religion, who after shee had made some good progresse therein, renounced publickly her countrey Idolatry, openly confessed her Christian faith, was, as she desired, baptised, and is since married to an English Gentleman of good vnderstanding, (as by his letter vnto me, containing the reasons for his marriage of her you may perceiue) an other knot to binde this peace the stronger.* Her Father, *and friends gaue approbation to it, and her Vncle gaue*

her

her to him in the Church: she liues ciuilly and louingly with him, and I trust will increase in goodnesse, as the knowledge of God increaseth in her. She will goe into England with me, and were it but the gayning of this one soule, I will thinke my time, toile, and present stay well spent.

Since this accident the Gouernours and people of Checkahomanies, *who are fiue hundred bow-men, and better, a stout and warlike Nation, haue made meanes to haue vs come vnto them, and conclude a peace, where all the Gouernours would meete me. They hauing thus three or foure times importuned mee, I resolued to goe; so taking Captain* Argall, *with fifty men in my frigot, and barge I went thither: Captaine* Argall *with forty men landed, I kept aboord for some reasons. Vpon the meeting they tould Captain* Argall *they had longed to be friends, that they had no* King, *but eight great men, who gouernd them. He tould them that we came to be friends, asked them if they would haue* King Iames *to be their* King, *& whether they would be his men? They after som conference between themselues, seemed willing of both, demaunding if we would fight against their enemies, he tould them that if any did them iniurie, they should send me word, and I would agree them, or if their aduersaries would not, then I would let them haue as many men as they would to help them: they liked well of that, and tould him that all their men should helpe vs. All this being agreed vpon,* C. Argall *gaue euery* Councellor *a* Tamahawk, *and a peece of Copper, which was kindly taken; they requested further, that if their*

their boats ſhould happen to meet with our boats, and that they ſaid they were the Chikahominy Engliſhmen, *and* King Iames *his men, we would let them paſſe: wee agreed vnto it, ſo that they pronounced them ſelues* Engliſh men, *and* King Iames *his men, promiſing within fifteen daies to come vnto* Iames *town to ſee me, and conclude theeſe conditions; euery bowman being to giue me as a* Tribute *to* King Iames *two meaſures of Corne euery harueſt, the two meaſures contayning two buſhells and a halfe, and I to giue euery bowman a ſmall* Tamahawke, *and to euery* Counſeller *a ſuit of red cloath, which did much pleaſe them. This people neuer acknowledged any* King, *before; no nor euer would acknowledge* Powhatan *for their* King, *a ſtout people they be, and a delicate ſeat they haue.*

Now Sir you ſee our conditions, you, and all worthy men may iudge, whether it would not be a griefe to ſee theſe faire hopes froſtbitten and theſe freſh budding plants to wither? which had I returned, had aſſuredly followed: for heer is no one that the people would haue to gouern them, but my ſelfe: for I had now come away, had I not found a generall deſire in the beſt ſort to returne for England: *letter vpon letter, requeſt vpon requeſt from their friends to returne, ſo as I knew not vpon whom to conferre the care of this buſines in my abſence. whom I thought fitte was generally diſtaſted, ſo as ſeeing the eminent enſuing danger, ſhould I haue left this multitude, not yet fully refined, I am reſolued to ſtay till harueſt be got in, and then ſettle things according to my poore vnderſtanding, and returne: if in the interim there come no authoriſed Gouernour from* England.

I *Conſi-*

Consider I pray you since things be brought to this passe as you see, and that I should haue come away, if then through their factions, humors, mutinies, *or indiscretion of the* Chiefes *I had left behind, this should fall to ruine: I then should receiue the imputation; I incurre the blame, for quitting the* Plantation, *although I might doe it, both with my honour, my promised stay of time being expired, and hauing warrant from my* Soueraigne, the Kings Maiesty: *but the precedent reasons moued me and that this action of such price, such excellency, and assured profit to mine own knowledge should not die to the scorne of our* Nation, *and to giue cause of laughter to the Papists that desire our ruine. I can assure you, no countrey of the world affoordes more assured hopes of infinit riches, which both by mine own peoples discouery, & the relation of such* Sauages, *whose fidelity we haue often found assureth me.*

Oh why should so many Princes, and noble men ingage themselues and therby intermedling herein, haue caused a number of soules transport themselues, and be transported hither? why should they (I say) relinquish this so glorious an Action: *for if their ends bee to build God a* Church, *they ought to perseuer: if othewise, yet their honour ingageth them to be constant. Howsoeuer they stand affected, heer is enough to content them, let their ends be either for* God, *or* Mammon.

These things haue animated me to stay for a little season, to leaue those, I am tied in conscience to returne vnto, to leaue the assured benefits of my other fortunes the sweete society of my friends, and acquaintance, with all mundall delightes, and reside heer with much turmoile, which I will constantly doe, rather then see Gods glorie diminished, my King *and Countrey*

trey dishonoured, and these poore people, I haue the charge of ruined. And so I beseech you to answere or me, if you heare me taxed for my staying, as some may iustly do, and that these are my chiefe motiues God *I take to vvitnesse. Remember me, and the cause I haue in hand, in your daily meditations, and reckon me in the number of those that doe sincerely loue you and yours, and vvill euer rest in all offices of a friend, to doe you seruice.*

From Iames towne in Virginia
the 18 of Iune, 1614.

Thomas Dale.

To my verie deere and louing *Cosen* M. G. *Minister of the* B. F. in London.

S*Ir the Colony here is much better. Sir* Thomas Dale *our religious and valiant Gouernour, hath now brought that to passe, which neuer before could be effected. For by vvarre vpon our enemies, and kinde vsage of our friends, he hath brought them to seeke for peace of vs, vvhich is made, and they dare not breake. But that vvhich is best, one* Pocahuntas *or* Matoa *the daughter of* Powhatan, *is married to an honest and discreete English Gentleman Maister* Rolfe, *and that after she had openly* *renounced her countrey Idolatry,confessed the faith of Iesus Christ,and vvas baptised; vvhich thing Sir* Thomas Dale *had laboured along time to ground in her.*

Yet notvvithstanding, are the vertuous deeds of this vvorthy Knight, much debased,by the letters vvhich some vvicked men haue vvritten from hence,and especially by one C. L. *If you heare any condemne this noble Knight, or doe feare to come hither, for those slaunderous letters, you may vpon my vvord bouldly reproue them. You knovv that no malefactors can abide the face of the Iudge, but themselues scorning to be reproued, doe prosecute vvith all hatred; all those that labour their amendment. I maruaile much that any men of honest life, should feare the sword of the magistrate, which is vnsheathed onely in their defence.*

Sir Thomas Dale (*vith vvhom I am*) *is a man of great knowledge in Diuinity,and of a good conscience in all his doings: both which bee rare in a martiall man. Euery Sabbath day wee preach in the forenoone, and Chatechize in the afternoone. Euery Saturday at night I exercise in Sir* Thomas Dales *house. Our Church affaires bee consulted on by the Minister, and foure of the most religious men. Once euery moneth wee haue a* Communion, *and once ayeer a solemn* Fast *For me,though my promis of 3 yeers seruice to my country be expired,yet I will abide in my vocation*

heere

here vntill I be lawfully called from hence. And so betaking vs all vnto the mercies of God in Christ Iesus, I rest for euer.

Virginia Iune 18. 1614.

Your most deere and louing cosen
Alex. Whitakers.

The coppie of the Gentle-mans letters to Sir *Thomas Dale*, that after maried *Powhatans daughter, containing the reasons mouing* him thereunto.

HOnourable Sir, and most vvorthy Gouerner: vvhen your leasure shall best serue you to peruse these lines, I trust in God, the beginning vvill not strike you into a greater admiration, then the end vvill giue you good content. It is a matter of no small moment, concerning my own particular which here I impart vnto you, and vvhich toucheth mee so neerely, as the tendernesse of my saluation. Howbeit I freely subiect my selfe to your graue and mature iudgement, deliberation, approbation and determination; assuring myselfe of your zealous admonitions, and godly comforts, either perswading me to desist, or incouraging me to persist therin, with a religious feare and godly care, for which (from the very instant, that this began to roote it selfe, vvithin the secret bosome of my brest) my daily and earnest praiers haue bin, still are, and euer shall be pro-

ed forthwith, as sincere, a godly zeale, as I possiblely may to be directed, aided and gouerned in all my thoughts, words and deedes, to the glory of God, and for my eternal consolation. To perseuere wherein I neuer had more neede, nor (till now) could euer imagine to haue bin moued with the like occasion.

But (my case standing as it doth) what better worldly refuge can I here seeke, then to shelter my selfe vnder the safety of your fauourable protection? And did not my case procede from an vnspotted conscience, I should not dare to offer to your view and aprroued iudgement, these passions of my troubled soule, so full of feare and trembling is hypocrisie and dissimulation. But knowing my owne innocency & godly feruor, in the whole prosecution hereof, I doubt not of your benigne acceptance, and clement construction. As for malicious deprauers, & turbulent spirits, to whom nothing is tastful, but what pleaseth their vnsauory pallat, I passe not for them being well assured in my perswasion (by the often triall and prouing of my selfe, in my holiest meditations and praiers) that I am called hereunto by the spirit of God; and it shall be sufficient for me to be protected by your selfe in all vertuous and pious indeuours. And for my more happie proceeding herein, my daily oblations shall euer be addressed to bring to passe so good effects, that your selfe, and all the world may truely say: This is the worke of God, and it is maruelous in our eies.

But to auoide tedious preambles, and to come neerer

neerer the matter: first suffer me vvith your patence, to svveepe and make cleane the way vvherein I vvalke, from all suspicions and doubts, vvhich may be couered therein, and faithfully to reueale vnto you, vvhat should moue me hereunto.

Let therefore this my vvell aduised protestation, vvhich here I make betweene God and my own conscience, be a sufficient vvitnesse, at the dreadfull day of iugdement (vvhen the secret of all mens harts shall be opened) to condemne me herein, if my chiefest intent and purpose be not, to striue with all my power of body and minde, in the undertaking of so mightie a matter, no vvay led (so farre forth as mans vveakenesse may permit) with the vnbridled desire of carnall affection: but for the good of this plantation, for the honour of our countrie, for the glory of God, for my owne saluation, and for the conuerting to the true knowledge of God and Iesus Christ, an vnbeleeuing creature, namely Pokahuntas. *To whom my hartie and best thoughts are, and haue a long time bin so intangled, and inthralled in so intricate a laborinth, that I vvas euen awearied to vnwinde my selfe thereout. But almighty God, vvho neuer faileth his, that truely inuocate his holy name hath opened the gate, and led me by the hand that I might plainely see and discerne the safe paths vvherein to treade.*

To you therefore (most noble Sir) the patron and Father of vs in this countrey doe I vtter the effects of this my setled and long continued affection (which

which hath made a mightie warre in my meditations) and here I doe truely relate, to what iſſue this dangerous combate is come vnto, wherein I haue not onely examined, but throughly tried and pared my thoughts euen to the quicke, befor I could finde any fit wholeſome and apt applications to cure ſo daungerous an vlcer. I neuer failed to offer my daily and faithfull praiers to God, for his ſacred and holy aſſiſtance. I forgot not to ſet before mine eies the frailty of mankinde, his prones to euill, his indulgencie of wicked thoughts, with many other imperfections wherein man is daily inſnared, and oftentimes ouerthrowne, and them compared to my preſent eſtate. Nor was I ignorant of the heauie diſpleaſure which almightie God conceiued againſt the ſonnes of Leuie *and* Iſrael *for marrying ſtrange wiues, nor of the inconueniences which may thereby ariſe, with other the like good motions which made me looke about warily and with good circumſpection, into the grounds and principall agitations, which thus ſhould prouoke me to be in loue with one whoſe education hath bin rude, her manners barbarous, her generation accurſed, and ſo diſcrepant in all nurtriture from my ſelfe, that oftentimes with feare and trembling, I haue ended my priuate controuerſie with this: ſurely theſe are wicked inſtigations, hatched by him who ſeeketh and delighteth in mans deſtruction; and ſo with feruent praiers to be euer preſerued from ſuch diabolical aſſaults (as I tooke thoſe to be) I haue taken ſome reſt.*

Thus

Thus when I had thought I had obtained my peace and quietnesse, beholde another, but more gracious tentation hath made breaches into my holiest and strongest meditations; with which I haue bin put to a new triall, in a straighter manner then the former: for besides the many passions and sufferings vvhich I haue daily, hourely, yea and in my sleepe indured, euen awaking mee to astonishment, taxing mee with remissnesse, and carelesnesse, refusing and neglecting to performe the duteie of a good Christian, pulling me by the eare, and crying: why dost not thou indeuour to make her a Christian? And these haue happened to my greater wonder, euen when she hath bin furthest seperated from me, which in common reason (were it not an vndoubted worke of God(might breede forgetfulnesse of a farre more worthie creature. Besides, I say the holy spirit of God hath often demaunded of me, why I was created? If not for transitory pleasures and worldly vanities, but to labour in the Lords vineyard, there to sow and plant, to nourish and increase the fruites thereof, daily adding with the good husband in the Gospell, somewhat to the tallent, that in the end the fruites may be reaped, to the comfort of the laborer in this life, and his saluation in the world to come? And if this be, as vndoubtedly this is, the seruice Iesus Christ requireth of his best seruant: wo vnto him that hath these instruments of pietie put into his hands, and wilfully despiseth to worke with them. Likewise, adding hereunto her great appa-

rance of loue to me, her desire to be taught and instructed in the knowledge of God, *her capablenesse of vndestanding, her aptnesse and willingnesse to receiue anie good impression, and also the spirituall, besides her owne incitements stirring me vp hereunto.*

What should I doe? shall I be of so vntoward a disposition, as to refuse to leade the blind into the right way? Shall I be so vnnaturall, as not to giue bread to the hungrie? or vncharitable, as not to couer the naked? Shall I despise to actuate these pious duties of a Christian? Shall the base feare of displeasing the world, ouerpower and withholde mee from reuealing vnto man these spirituall workes of the Lord, which in my meditations and praiers, I haue daily made knowne vnto him? God for bid, I assuredly trust hee hath thus delt with me for my eternall felicitie, and for his glorie: and I hope so to be guided by his heauenly graice, that in the end by my faithfull paines, and christianlike labour, I shall attaine to that blessed promise, Pronounced by that holy Prophet Daniell *vnto the righteous that bring many vnto the knowledge of God. Namely, that they shall shine like the starres forever and eur. A sweeter comfort cannot be to a true Christian, nor a greater incouragement for him to labour all the daies of his life, in the performance thereof, nor a greater gaine of consolation, to be desired at the hower of death, and in the day of iudgement.*

Againe by my reading, and conference vvith honeſt and religious perſons, haue I receiued no ſmall encouragement, beſides ſerena mea conſcientia, *the cleereneſſe of my conſcience, clean from the filth of impurity,* quæ eſt inſtar muri ahenei, *vvhich is vnto me, as a braſen vvall. If I ſhould ſet down at large, the perturbations & godly motions, which haue ſtriuen vvithin mee, I ſhould but make a tedious & vnneceſſary volume. But I doubt not theſe ſhall be ſufficient both to certifie you of my tru intents, in diſcharging of my dutie to God, & to your ſelfe, to vvhoſe gracious prouidence I humbly ſubmit my ſelfe, for his glory, your honour, our Countreys good, the benefit of this Plantation, and for the conuerting of one vnregenerate, to regeneration; vvhich I beſeech God to graunt, for his deere Sonne Chriſt Ieſus his ſake.*

Now if the vulgar ſort, who ſquare all mens actions by the baſe rule of their own filthineſſe, ſhall taxe or taunt me in this my godly labour: let them know, it is not any hungry appetite, to gorge my ſelfe vvith incontinency; ſure (if I would, and were ſo ſenſually inclined) I might ſatisfie ſuch deſire, though not vvithout a ſeared conſcience, yet vvith Chriſtians more pleaſing to the eie, and leſſe feareful in the offence vnlawfully committed. Nor am I in ſo deſperate an eſtate, that I regard not what becommeth of mee; nor am I out of hope but one day to ſee my Country, nor ſo void of friends, nor mean in birth, but there to obtain a mach to my great con-

tent: nor haue I ignorantly passed ouer my hopes there, or regardlesly seek to loose the loue of my friends, by taking this course: I know them all, and haue not rashly ouerslipped any.

But shal it please God thus to dispose of me (which I earnestly desire to fullfill my ends before sette down) I vvill heartely accept of it as a godly taxe appointed me, and I will neuer cease, (God assisting me) vntill I haue accomplished, & brought to perfection so holy a vvorke, in which I vvill daily pray God to blesse me, to mine, and her eternall happines. And thus desiring no longer to liue, to enioy the blessings of God, then this my resolution doth tend to such godly ends, as are by me before declared: not doubting of your fauourable acceptance, I take my leaue, beseeching Almighty God to raine downe vpon you, such plenitude of his heauenly graces, as your heart can wish and desire, and so I rest,

At your commaund most willing
to be disposed off

Iohn Rolfe.

Virginia therefore standing now in such a goodly proportion, and faire forwardnesse of thriuing, as it was neuer yet hitherto seen in, since it began to be first planted: cannot but soone come to perfection, to the exceeding great comfort of all well affected Christians,

Chriſtians, and no ſmall profit of the planters, and aduenturers: if it be well ſeconded and ſupplyed, with a good number of able men: Wherefore, let none bee heerafter vnwilling all they may to further this moſt honourable Action, and be forward to vphold and ſupport it from falling, by their ſpeech, and countenance, and freely aduenturing thither, both in their perſons, & alſo by their purſes, as God hath inabled them. To conclude, as *Azariah* ſayd once to King *Azah, Iuda*, and *Beniamin*, ſo ſay I vnto all. *Bee yee ſtrong threfore, and let not your hands be weake: for your worke ſhall haue a reward.* And as the holy Apoſtle ſaid to the Corinthians, *Be yee therefore ſtedfaſt, vnmoueable, abundant alwaies in the vvorkes of the Lord, for as much as ye know your labour is not in vaine in the Lord; let vs not therefore bee vvearie of vvelldoing:* for in due ſeaſon, *vvee ſhall reape*, if wee faint not as the Apoſtle tolde the Galatians. Farewell.

FINIS.

Errata.

Pag. 5. line 3 3. hir. p. 10. l.96 *Opichenkano.* p. 15. l.14 Weroance. p. 17. l. 22. manure. p. 17, l. 34. next to vs, read ſo as if. p. 18. l.4. halfe. p. 18.l. 8. as. p. 18. l. 12. purpoſed. p. 11. l. 16. diuers. p. 21. l. 27 Saine. p. 22. l. 21. after *doth* read, not. p. 23. l. 13, leaue out, he. p. 24. l. 16, cure. p. 27. l. 24. bring. p: 31, l. 2. read immediatelie after by name, Coxendale: and after the word, *called*, read, Hope in and. p. 21. l. 25, Somer. p. 42. l. 24. luring. p. 45. l. 1. read, after diſcontentment, went. p. 46. l. 11. meſſengers. p. 47, l. 11 perſonally

www.ingramcontent.com/pod-product-compliance
Lightning Source LLC
Chambersburg PA
CBHW020333090426
42735CB00009B/1518

* 9 7 8 3 3 3 7 2 2 2 4 2 0 *